READY, SET, GO!

The Start-Up Guide for Opening, Remodeling, & Running a Successful Beauty Salon

By Jeff Grissler & Eric Ryant

2012 Edition

"I loved the Ready, Set, Go! book! In fact, when I read it, I found myself wishing I had a book like this 30 years ago when I first started my business. Instead, I suffered through the process of doing it all on my own and learning the hard way—through trial and error. I'm pleased to see that salon owners will have a manual and a roadmap that insures the success of their salon business and their dreams.

This book is a pivotal tool in strengthening our industry one salon at a time. It is obvious that Jeff and Eric took great care and thoroughly covered everything salon owners need to consider when opening, remodeling, or expanding their business. They are industry experts and know the salon business better than most. Jeff and Eric have broken down and made the plan for success easy to implement. They share knowledge, wisdom, and the keys to success.

What a great contribution Jeff and Eric have made to the industry, as well as to new and veteran salon owners, through this priceless book."

Geno Stampora – Consultant & Speaker

Ready, Set, Go! The Start-Up Guide for Opening, Remodeling, & Running a Successful Beauty Salon
© 2012 Jeff Grissler and Eric Ryant. All Rights Reserved.

First edition.

Published in the U.S. by Ready Set Go Publishing, LLC
215 Pascal Street
Fort Collins Colorado 80524

Printed in the United States of America

ISBN 978-0-615-56358-9
Library of Congress Control Number 2014907596

About the Authors

Jeff Grissler has been where you are and understands the inner workings of the salon industry and what leads to success as a salon owner. As a business owner, he understands the business landscape and what owners can expect and guides them to success. Jeff is a partner of and the National Sales Manager for Quest Resources—one of the salon industry's leading financing companies for furniture and equipment. His career in finance began on Wall Street and he has been involved in the multimillion dollar beauty industry for over 20 years. Jeff has financed over 15,000 salons to help them open their doors or complete their remodeling project through creative financing strategies.

Published in many beauty trade magazines, Jeff is setting a new business standard in the beauty industry as we see it today. Jeff has a beauty portfolio of over 600 million dollars in salon financing and a network of over 150 manufacturers, distributors, and vendors. A gifted businessman and consultant, Jeff prides himself on his networking ability to bring people together to share new ideas and explore partnerships and marketing techniques. Through his skilled negotiations, he has convinced the banking industry to lift restrictions from the beauty industry. He has also negotiated contracts and leases with salon owners, spa owners, distributors, manufacturers, and banking management.

Jeff was born in New York City before moving to the Jersey Shore. He was a New York City fireman for 15+ years and served during 911. Jeff now resides in Wilmington, NC with his wife, Coleen, and their three children—Kaytlyn, JT, and Julianna Rose.

Jeff offers consulting services to current salon owners and to those who have salon ownership in their near-term or future career plans. To reach Jeff, you can contact him directly at to jgrissler@questrs.com.

Eric Ryant is a beauty industry entrepreneur with over 30 years of experience in space-planning and design for salons. No stranger to the salon industry, Eric spent many years developing new designs and space plans, getting involved in every facet of the industry. Since the 1980s, Eric has imported salon furniture from many countries, such as Italy, Germany, Holland, and China, bringing in the latest trends and styles for the U.S. market.

Prior to writing this book, Eric owned several successful businesses, all involved in the salon industry, from a small chain of beauty stores to a cabinet manufacturing facility. He has also collaborated with companies such as Sally Beauty Supply, L'Oreal, and The Nailco Group.

Eric's vision is to help clients create their dream salon with a cost-effective business model and ensure that they stay within budget for the long haul. As part of his successful career, he now teaches and consults with other organizations on how to achieve the same success. Eric can be reached at ericryant@gmail.com.

Acknowledgements

Jeff Grissler

You never really understand how important your friends and family are until you take on a large project. My wife, Coleen, was my sounding board and always had insightful feedback. I can't tell you how much I appreciated her support and encouragement. My children, Kaytlyn, JT, and Julianna are always an inspiration and fill my life with joy.

Eric Ryant

First and foremost, I want to thank my wife, Wendi, for planting the seed to write this book. She is an amazing woman and I am fortunate to have her by my side. Thanks for believing in me. To my children, Chase, Kendall, and Sloane, and my stepchildren, Daniel and Cory, just know that anything is possible and writing this book is proof of it. If you put your mind to it, you can accomplish anything.

INTRODUCTION

The Beauty Industry Today—As We See It

The haircare industry is a multibillion dollar business. The economic climate has never had a big impact on products and services. Salons have survived during all financial and economic climates and circumstances.

The beauty industry has grown faster than most businesses, due to people's perception of themselves and the importance they place on looking and feeling their best. The world is ever-changing, and the beauty industry has evolved from Baby Boomer styles to Generation X. We, as a society, love new trends and the ability to create them.

We have always been a vain society. Vanity has been an important factor for the beauty industry. The look-good, feel-good way of living is more apparent in the world of today than ever before. As we age, the importance of keeping a young, healthy look has become an everyday way of life—and an obsession to some. Anti-aging products are an industry unto themselves. The beauty industry will continue to be at the forefront, keeping the world looking young and feeling beautiful.

Even in today's difficult economic conditions, our industry will continue to grow and prosper. People need the beauty industry. Women entering the workplace and climbing the corporate ladder have been the most crucial driving force behind the explosion of sales in the beauty industry for the past decade. Women of all ages and economic backgrounds are relying on the services of the beauty industry to create and maintain their image—whatever that image may be.

Men's vanity and egos, now unbridled, are bringing them to salons on a more frequent basis. Men-only salons are now in most cities. It is now more common for men to get color treatments in salons. These changes, as well as other related salon and spa services for men, will continue to grow. The job market for the middle-aged man is highly competitive; they need to rely on monthly salon visits to keep looking young, as well as looking good.

Products related to hair color, makeup, and skincare will continue to evolve. The manufacturers of these products will continue to transform full-service salons into epicenters for the education, services, and mass distribution of these products worldwide.

It is apparent that the need for beauty-related products and services will continue to progress as we try to prolong the aging process and seek new styles, products, and services to keep us looking young and beautiful.

All of this is very good news for the entrepreneur in the salon business. You have a great opportunity to prosper because this is one of the few industries where demand actually meets supply. The magnitude of products is overwhelming but still constantly growing. Full-service salons have great business potential.

Ready, Set Go! is the most comprehensive business-building guide in the beauty industry today. We have years of industry experience and knowledge to guide you through the process of starting or remodeling your salon business. Quotes from salon owners from all over the world are found in the "Salon Owner/Operators Discuss the Good, the Bad, & the Ugly" comments section. You will hear salon owners discuss their success and failure stories from their own experiences.

Starting, renovating, or expanding a business is a big decision. We want to make sure that you have the right tools that can guide you to success and give you the information you need to save you from potential hardships and stress of financial losses.

This book will assist you to form the right business structure, build an effective location with the proper space-planning ideas, align with equipment and product manufacturers, and create good education and hiring techniques and business practices, all with a good business model in place. We will help you set your intentions and allow you to follow through with your dream of successful salon ownership. Ready, Set, Go! is more than a textbook—it will become the heartbeat of your salon and allow you financial independence when building and growing your business.

TABLE OF CONTENTS

CHAPTER 1

Getting Started

"He who is not courageous enough to take risks will accomplish nothing in life."

—Muhammad Ali

At some point in your life, you probably experienced a wishful child who has set up a lemonade stand—maybe that child was you or one of your own children. What do you think the purpose was behind setting up that lemonade stand? I bet it wasn't so that they could meet the neighbors. That child saw the lemonade stand as their opportunity to make money. Now, most parents will squash the idea of a lemonade stand. Why? Because they've experienced it in some shape or form during their lifetime. They'll warn their little one of all the challenges, the hard work, and the slim odds of being able to make money.

However, a handful of these young entrepreneurs will follow through with their idea of opening a lemonade stand. They've seen other kids do it; so why can't they do it too? They will work hard to make their signs, set up their stand, and make their pitchers of lemonade. Then, most will sit and wait for cars to drive by or for people to walk by and buy their delicious, ice-cold lemonade.

Think about the last time you drove by a lemonade stand. Did you see children patiently waiting for their customers? Or, were they frantically waving their arms and signs and trying to grab your attention? Most of the time, I see frantic displays and attempts to get my attention when I drive by a child's lemonade stand.

As you can imagine, many a lemonade stand will open and close in one day. And the child who thought they could make money by selling lemonade will realize that it wasn't as easy as they thought. But, what if they would have studied the market a bit more? What if they would have made fresh-squeezed lemonade? What if they would have considered different locations for their stand, like a local farmer's market, their school's baseball field, or in a neighborhood that was holding a local art festival event?

The more planning that goes behind opening a business, even one as small as a lemonade stand, can increase the odds of success.

However, you must not fool yourself and we don't want you to walk into this without the full picture of what it takes to open or renovate a salon. It's a fact that the salon industry has one of the highest rates of business failure. Opening a salon and investing in a renovation or relocation project, takes planning, capital, and business management skills. For some salons, the profit is so small that the salon owners make the same amount of money that they did when they worked for someone else. Only now, they have the additional responsibilities and pressure of being a business owner.

Making the decision to open a salon is complex and presents huge questions that you may be tossing around in your head, such as:

- Where do I begin?
- What is the first step?
- Who do I talk to?
- Where do I find the staff?
- Why do I want to do this?

- Is the risk worth the reward?
- Do I want all the responsibilities?
- Do I have enough capital?
- Do I have the management skills?
- Do I have the ability?

As you can see, there are so many questions and so many different aspects to consider. You will not only be cutting hair, but managing people, purchasing product, marketing your business—the list of new duties and responsibilities goes on and on.

But, we are here to tell you—everyone has the ability and all it takes is planning and guidance.

Ready, Set, Go! is a guide to assist you in making your dreams come true. This book is meant to prepare you mentally for what you can expect as a salon owner, how to get a handle on the financial obligations, and help you properly plan and navigate the process of opening, renovating, and expanding your salon business so that you have a greater chance for success. We are going to take you through a step-by-step process to give you concepts and guidance that will sustain a long-term, profitable operation. In the end, the purpose for owning and operating your salon business is to make money, right?

Can You Beat the Odds?

The Cosmetologists of America (COA) is a national salon industry organization that says that there are 1,680,000 professional stylists, estheticians, nail techs, and barbers in the USA. Approximately 500,000 salons incorporate all of these professions. Of these, 850,000 personal appearance workers held jobs in their related field in 2010. According to many business magazines, the cosmetology profession is one of the fastest-growing, most desirable industries in the nation today.

From an overall industry standpoint, these figures look great. Over the years, we've found that almost all business failures can be attributed to poor management or a lack of capital or experience. In most cases, the salon owner:

- Opened in an area crowded with competing salons
- Did not offer services that the market wanted or needed
- Did not change when local market conditions changed
- Did not have sufficient capital to sustain the business
- Lacked knowledge or experience in these matters:
    1. Accounting
    2. Understanding profit margins
    3. Employee relations
    4. Finances
    5. Marketing for this type of business
    6. Purchasing and retailing

A lack of knowledge results in the inability to come up with the right answers when faced with operating decisions. That is why some entrepreneurs leaving cosmetology school look for a franchise as a way to open up their first salon business. Many franchises offer training programs, ongoing management assistance, and a proven track record of success. While franchises are not guaranteed, the percentage of success is much greater than independent startups that learn by trial and error.

So, before deciding to open a salon, you have to make a commitment to doing what it will take to be successful. It may all sound good in your mind, but there are many factors to consider and questions you must ask yourself to decide if this is really something you want to do.

Deciding Factors

Let's look at the deciding factors that will help you determine whether you are ready to open your own salon business.

Start by looking at the pros and cons of owning and operating your own salon.

	PRO	CON
1	You get to make all the decisions.	When the decision is wrong, you have to live with the consequences.
2	You get to create the client or guest experience that you want.	You must lead others with your vision to help them provide this experience.
3	You can decorate and furnish the salon to your liking.	You have to pay for it out of your own financial capital and stick to your budget.
4	You can open a salon close to where you live.	If there are too many salons in the area where you live, you will have to look elsewhere.
5	You'll have employees working for you.	Your employees are relying on you to run a successful business and help with their growth and development.

Next, consider your experience: Have you worked long enough in a salon setting?

Working for someone else gives you an overall sense of what goes on in a salon each day. When you graduate cosmetology school, you normally will not have the business experience to own and operate a salon. Creativity alone does not ensure you will be a successful salon owner. The benefit of working in a salon allows you the time to grow as a person, build your client base, and learn from your mistakes while working and getting paid by someone else. We recommend that you get a job in a salon that is in the geographical area in which you want to eventually open your business.

Do you have the business management experience to run a salon?

Having the proper education in beauty techniques is vital to your success, but you cannot overlook the fact that you will have to have the ability to use a computer proficiently and also have a basic understanding of marketing, accounting, and finance. We suggest that you take a few computer and business courses at a local community college to learn the skills needed to run your business. Understanding the bottom line is critical to success.

Are You Ready?

The next step is to ask yourself some questions about your current situation, your job, and your financial position.

Look at your current job and ask yourself:

○ Does your job give you a good retirement plan, health insurance, and vacation?

○ Do you like the security of working for someone and is that more important to you than owning your own salon?

○ Are you afraid of risk?

○ Do you think you can make more money if you open your own business?

○ Do you have the business management skills to run a business?

○ Do you have basic computer skills?

○ Have you had experience managing people?

○ Can you envision what success looks like and get other people on board to help you fulfill your vision?

○ Do you manage yourself well during times of stress or uncertainty?

Remember, when you open your business, everything becomes your responsibility and your decisions and your actions will affect not only you, but your staff as well.

If you find that you are indeed satisfied with your current job or that you still need more experience, then this book will assist you on your career potential in the industry. You can begin setting the foundation for salon ownership in the future.

However, if you have found that you have what it takes to start your own salon business, then read on. You will find that this book is the most comprehensive learning guide for getting ready to embark on building a successful salon.

One stylist/owner told us how she knew she was ready: "When I had too many clients to handle on my own, even after working a 14-hour day four times a week."

Entrepreneurial Self-Test

To help you decide if opening your salon is truly the right move for you, take this test. Answer honestly and figure out your score based on the information given below to assist you in uncovering more information about yourself and your abilities to own and operate a successful salon.

Please rate these questions 1 to 5 (1 being lowest and 5 highest)

1. I seek opportunities all the time.	1	2	3	4	5
2. I look toward the future, not the past.	1	2	3	4	5
3. I am committed to being the best.	1	2	3	4	5
4. I am market-driven and customer-oriented.	1	2	3	4	5
5. I value employees and I am willing to develop them.	1	2	3	4	5
6. I am tolerant of small tasks.	1	2	3	4	5
7. I don't accept failure.	1	2	3	4	5
8. I am realistic.	1	2	3	4	5
9. I am decisive and focused.	1	2	3	4	5
10. I have business management experience.	1	2	3	4	5

Scoring Breakdown

1. If you score less than 25 points, we recommend that you get a job in a progressive, growing salon in your area which will set the stage to take this test again in a year.

2. If your score is between 25 and 35 points, we recommend that you concentrate on your work ethic and take some more courses on self-development or business.

3. If your score is more than 35 points, you may be ready to take the next step. There is no guarantee, but the opportunity to succeed with drive and determination is a possibility.

It is important to realize that this test is just one way of knowing whether you have the motivation and drive to start your own business. You need to realize that the current world is a quick-paced, ever-changing market and what worked well yesterday may not work well today. As a business owner, you must be a good listener and learner, always open to new ideas and concepts. Success comes from doing everything well rather than just doing a few things exceptionally well.

As Tom Smith, president of Food Lion grocery stores stated, *"We don't try to be 1000 percent better on a few things; we try to be one percent better on 1000 things."*

You have to be better. And to be better, you must have the courage, ability, and the commitment to your business and your customers.

CHAPTER 2

The American Dream

"Going into business for yourself, becoming an entrepreneur, is the modern-day equivalent of pioneering on the old frontier."
—Paula Nelson

The American Dream is about building a better life for yourself and having the opportunity to succeed based on your aspirations and your abilities. Most people fulfill this dream through their careers or business ownership.

Millions of Americans will choose to go to work for a company that will provide regular paychecks, a sense of security, health insurance, retirement savings plans, etc. While many will be content working for someone else, others will dream of owning and running their own business. Is this you? Do you want something more out of your job and career?

One thing is for certain, the American Dream is still possible. Just like the early pioneers setting out to find new farmland, you have to get over your fear of the unknown and you have to be willing to commit yourself to your dream of a better life. And, for those of you currently working for someone else, you have to ready yourselves for the loss of a regular paycheck.

Over 600,000 new businesses opened all over the country last year. Excited entrepreneurs of all ages did exactly what they needed to do to start their business. They planned, plotted, borrowed, and invested so that they could open and build their own successful business. Many are winning, doing well, making a profit, and living the life of an entrepreneur.

What makes these people different? Do they have a crystal ball that allows them to predict the future or is it that they see things differently than most people?

New entrepreneurs simply look at the economy and figure out a way to take the best advantage of the opportunity that exists. The new entrepreneurs are finding solutions and reshaping the way people did business in the past so that it's successful in the present and

7

positioned for the future. They are showing people in the world that they can open a business, buy a building, hire people, and operate a business.

Have you decided that owning a business and being an entrepreneur is your destiny? If your answer is, "YES!," then, we would like to be the first to say, "Congratulations!" You have made your first step and you are on your way.

In the next chapter, you will see the checklist for turning your dream of salon ownership into a reality. But, before we do that, let's take a minute to really describe your dream so that you can see it in your mind's eye. This will be helpful when things get stressful; and, they **will** get stressful. So, you want to be very grounded in your dream and aware of why you are setting out on this adventure.

This is My Dream …

When I close my eyes and imagine my salon:

I see …	
I hear …	
I feel …	

I want to open a salon because:

○ I want to have the best salon in the area.

○ I would like to educate and develop the best salon team in the country.

○ Creating is my life.

○ People will come to my place of business because they feel welcome.

○ Color is my life.

○ Living, loving, and education are my focus and my life.

○ I want my customers to look good and feel good about their hair.

When clients come to my salon for the first time, they will:

Say …	
Feel …	
Think …	

Employees of my salon will:

Say …	
Feel …	
Think …	

Remember, in life, it is up to you to create your own destiny and fulfill your dreams. But, you can't just dream, you must do!

CHAPTER 3

New Business Checklist

"There is not another professional alliance that comes close to the one between a woman and her hairstylist. Her doctor sees her once a year if she's healthy and not pregnant. Her shrink is generally more expensive and not nearly as cheery. Her personal trainer? Too sweaty; too bossy. A hairdress holds a trusted place in a woman's life."

—Linda Wells, Editor in Chief, Allure Magazine

Before you run out and actually hang a shingle and announce the opening of your new salon, you must carefully plan your startup business venture. You need to begin by making decisions. You will have to determine how big you actually want your salon to be, the types of services you will offer, and whether the salon is a full-service salon with nail care, makeup, and other spa-type services. These added services may require finding a larger location and all the expenses that go along with that—from equipment and furniture to product and staff.

The average salon in the U.S. is 1200 square feet with six operators. If you add services, it could mean you may need as much as 3000 square feet. Before you invest your time and money blindly, always put your vision and financial budget on paper.

In order to fulfill your vision or dream, you will need the following:

- Money or financial backing
- A comprehensive business plan
- Conceptual site plan design and salon layout
- Equipment and furniture evaluation and supplies
- Budgets, including costs associated with startup, construction, equipment, furniture, and six months to a years' worth of operating expenses

Breaking down your initial startup costs is also important. The amount of money you will need to get your business up and running is not an easy task to figure out. Consider these factors.

Initial Startup Costs

Begin by estimating the expenses you will incur when first opening your business:

- Salon furniture and equipment
- Spa furniture and equipment
- Office and backroom (tables, chairs, refrigerator, washer/dryer, desks, filing cabinets, etc.)
- Computer system equipment (desktops/laptops/tablets, printers/scanners/fax machines, modem/Internet)
- Signage (outdoor/indoor)
- Phone system (phones and phone lines)
- Sound system
- Lighting
- Display cases
- Reception furniture
- Initial product purchase
- Televisions (if needed)

Don't forget construction costs. Construction overruns can be the death of any salon startup. The building and setup costs of any new business will be the most expensive thing you do as a new business owner. Moving into any space may mean changes: plumbing, electrical, carpentry, flooring, handicap-accessible bathrooms, and heating/air conditioning will be costly and never seem to come in on budget. Always add an extra 20% when figuring your expense. That should cover any unexpected costs.

Salon Owner/Operators Discuss the Good, the Bad, & the Ugly

Fever Hair Design, Tannin

"Thinking that the construction would only take 30 days, simply because that's what the contractor told me. Then, I watched it drag out to 90 days (and double in cost) while I went without income!"

If you are opening, renovating, or expanding a salon that will include spa services, remember to include massage tables, skincare machines, pedicure units, and hydrotherapy units. If you are looking into medical spa services, those machines require additional insurance and are extremely costly. Most items for spas are significantly higher than normal salon equipment.

Other one-time charges include:

- Deposits for public utilities
- Deposits for your building lease
- Installation of phone and computer lines
- Licenses and permits
- Professional and accounting fees
- First-year premium for business insurance policy
- Initial order of products needed for retail, dispensary, and back bar

You will have a better understanding of your startup costs by doing some simple things, such as looking at equipment online, checking out catalogs, going to a local beauty trade show, speaking to a salon designer, and calling utility companies for an estimated payment for your space. Speak to your potential vendors, accountants, and contractors. All of these things will give you estimates on your monthly overhead. All of this should be done before you begin the next step—finding a location. Make sure these costs are within your budget.

Owner Salary & Payroll

Chances are your startup business will not immediately generate enough revenue to cover all your expenses plus payroll and salary. Therefore, you will need to add your startup costs plus monthly expenses in order to allocate funds for personal expenses.

Depending on your circumstances, and how much money you have put aside for your new business, it could take anywhere from a few months to a year before your business will be able to pay you a salary. If you plan for this, you will not panic after six months when you still don't have enough income to draw a salary. You must always plan conservatively when forecasting salary projections.

Get Organized

This chapter involves breaking down the different parts that are essential for creating a successful business model. By following this guide, it will help you focus on all the issues that need to be addressed in the beginning or planning stages.

We suggest you buy a large binder and a set of tabs. You can use them to organize all of your paperwork and ideas for your new salon. Create a nice cover for your binder with your salon name and logo. This is a motivational and empowering way to get started.

Here are the tabs that you need to create for your binder and the types of information that you will start adding to it.

1. Location
2. Business plan
3. Incorporation
4. Financial & Accounting
5. Operational
6. Website
7. Risk Management
8. Revenue
9. Branding/Marketing
10. Furniture & Equipment

Location

1. Print out maps and check out the competition in the area
2. Take pictures
3. Research lease and/or purchase costs
4. Write down or find out contact information for leasing or real estate agent
5. Find at least three locations

Business Plan

1. Create a business plan
2. Capital investment
3. Forecasting, goals, revenue streams
4. Executive Summary

Incorporation

1. Incorporate business
2. Occupational license
3. Create legal business documents, including articles of incorporation
4. Buy-Sell Agreements
5. Open business checking account
6. Agree on partner capital investment

7. Fictitious name registration
8. Obtain business license
9. Obtain EIN (Employment Identification Number)
10. Review all laws for the license and registration requirements

Financial/Accounting

1. Establish payment methods—credit cards, PayPal™, finance options
2. Terms and conditions of payment through suppliers
3. Billing, accounts payable, inventory, salon software
4. Create detailed financial projections
5. Explore Small Business Administration (SBA) loans, grants, and other available governmental subsidies

Operational

1. Assign duties and responsibilities
2. Number of employees and positions needed
3. Necessary supplies needed for budget
4. Create relationship with preferred shipper (UPS, FedEx®)
5. Employee training, handbook
6. Payroll program or ADP, a company that provides Automatic Data Processing

Website

1. Conceptualize purpose and layout of Web presence
2. Hire Web designer/manager
3. Create domain
4. Email addresses
5. Evaluate and determine best Web resources for product sales (eBay, Craig's List)

Risk Management

1. Business insurance
2. Insurance on property and equipment
3. Legal agreements with suppliers
4. Umbrella policy

Revenue

1. Create catalog of merchandise
2. Establish pricing and GM methodology for both retail and distribution

Branding/Marketing

1. Secure the services of a brand expert if you are having trouble coming up with a name and a logo for your salon
2. Letterhead and paper supplies, business cards, salon menu
3. Set up phones
4. Create an overall marketing strategy and company logos. Be sure to include social media marketing strategies, using tools like Facebook, YouTube, Twitter, Foursquare, Groupon, Google+, and LinkedIn.

Furniture & Equipment

1. Salon furniture
2. Salon equipment
3. Office equipment & furniture: copiers, computers, networking

CHAPTER 4

How to Pick the Right Location

"A dream doesn't become reality through magic, it takes sweat, determination, and hard work."

—Colin Powell

It is said the three most important decisions you will make are location, location, and location. If you are creating and building your first salon or even relocating or opening a second location, then the details of the location might not be the first thing on your mind, but they SHOULD be.

Put location on the top of your list as the single most important factor for your new business. Your amazing concepts, services, and products will go unnoticed if you do not take the time to do your homework and pinpoint the perfect location. Your location is a huge factor in how you market your business, determine which products to carry, and set prices for services. Your location says a lot about you, your salon, your brand, and the customers you wish to attract.

Here are several key factors that you should consider when choosing your salon/retail location:

Population & Your Customer

Begin by researching the city and area you have selected for your salon thoroughly before making a final decision. Read local papers and speak to the small business owners in the region. Ask them the difficult questions regarding their business: "What unexpected expenses, like taxes and fees, came up when you started your business here? Is the Chamber of Commerce active in promoting new businesses? Is the city or county good at repairing the streets, sidewalks, etc. on which your business is located?"

Obtain location demographics from the library, online, Chamber of Commerce and/or the Census Bureau. The best advice you will receive is from the local coffee shop or restaurants in the neighborhood. Observe the people: how do they dress, where do they shop, when are people shopping, and are they buying.

Accessibility, Visibility, & Traffic

Don't confuse a lot of traffic for a lot of customers. Your salon wants to be in a location where there are many shoppers, but only if the shopper meets the definition of your target market. Small retail stores may benefit from the traffic of nearby larger stores. When considering visibility, look at the location from the customer's viewpoint to answer these questions. In many cases, the better visibility your salon has, the less advertising needed. A freestanding building on the outskirts of town will need more marketing dollars than the salon located in a mall or on a main street.

These questions will give you more insight on picking your location.

✓ **CHECK IT OUT**

Location, Location, Location

How many people walk or drive past the location in a given day, week, or month?

Day _____   Week _____   Month _____

Is the area served by public transportation? ○ Yes ○ No

Is it lit up and safe at night? ○ Yes ○ No

Can clients easily get in and out of the parking lot? ○ Yes ○ No

Is there adequate parking? ○ Yes ○ No

Does this location have 10 parking spots for every 1000 square feet of space? ○ Yes ○ No

If the location is off a busy street or highway, is it easy to get to? ○ Yes ○ No

Is there adequate fire and police presence in the community? ○ Yes ○ No

What is the crime rate in the neighborhood? ○ Yes ○ No

Can the store be seen from the main flow of traffic? ○ Yes ○ No

Will the salon's sign be visible? ○ Yes ○ No

Is there easy access to the salon? ○ Yes ○ No

If there is a divider on the main street, would clients have to make a U-turn? ○ Yes ○ No

Signage, Zoning, & Planning

Before you enter into a lease or purchase agreement, be sure you understand all the rules, policies, and procedures related to your salon location. Contact the local city hall and Zoning Commission for information on regulations regarding the space you are interested in. The planning board determines the correct use for the location. Although the landlord may love the idea of having a full-service salon in that location, the planning board will have the final say on whether or not it is allowed.

It also may be a good idea to ask the planning officer about signage and regulations. Many towns are very sensitive about the height and the type of signage allowed.

Competition & Neighbors

When choosing your location, it is a good idea to see how many salons are in the same vicinity as the location you are interested in. Other types of businesses may help or hurt your business. The key is to be next to a retailer that draws other people to the area. Schools, hospitals, and large stores are also a big draw in small towns. Being next to a busy coffee shop or designer store may be fantastic to give you instant exposure. Being next to a muffler shop or a business that is very loud or uses all the available parking will be a major deterrent.

Location Costs

Besides the base rent, consider all the costs involved when choosing your salon location. These costs will be your monthly overhead no matter what else arises:

- Lawn care, building maintenance, utilities, and security
- Upkeep and repair of the heating/air conditioning units
- Average utility bill
- Property taxes (depending on the lease)
- Water and sewer costs
- Insurance on the property and contents

Personal Factors

If you are going to be in the salon on a daily basis, think about your personal factors. How far would the salon be from your home and other things you do on a daily basis? Do you need to take children to school? How close is your bank? How far is shopping? The commute can easily overshadow the exhilaration of your new business if you are spending a lot of time traveling to and from work. Commuting has the potential to stifle your independence.

Questions That Will Make or Break Your Location

Following is a list of questions you should answer before choosing your salon's location.

Most people focus their energy on the creative side of the new business and neglect some important aspects of choosing a location. Answering these questions for the site you are considering will help you determine if you have chosen the right location for your new business.

Check off the questions below as you get answers.

○ Is the facility located in an area that is zoned for a salon?

○ Is the facility large enough for your business?

○ Does it meet your layout requirements?

○ Does the building need repairs?

○ Does the building have a crawl space or basement for easy access to utilities?

○ Are the lease terms and rent favorable?

○ Is the location convenient to where you live?

○ Can you find qualified employees?

○ Does the location have the customers you are looking for?

○ Is this a seasonal community?

○ Does the area have the image you are looking for?

○ Is this a safe neighborhood?

○ Is there exterior lighting on the building?

○ Will local business attract clients to your salon?

○ Are there many competitors nearby?

○ Can suppliers make deliveries conveniently at this location?

○ Is the parking adequate for the salon?

○ Is the area served by public transportation?

○ Can potential clients see the location at night?

○ Will there be walk-in business?

Salon Owner/Operators
Discuss the Good,
the Bad, & the Ugly

Suzanne Thompson Mills

"Not negotiating enough square footage! We have been in the salon for a year and within the first three months had outgrown our space and continue to grow ... other than that, I have no regrets or mistakes that I haven't been able to learn from and turn around to our benefit."

Kim Titu, Pontello

"I started small, wasn't paying for square footage that wasn't producing income. 1000 square feet kept it small and cozy until growth required more space. Then moved into a much larger space: too big, too quick, and too expensive."

Nikki Cameron, Salon Owner/Operator

"Not researching the location enough. And, I would have interviewed and hired before opening. [It would have been] a lot less headache and given me a little more time to know the staff before working with them."

CHAPTER 5

How to Negotiate Your Lease

"To create something exceptional, your mindset must be relentlessly focused on detail."

—Giorgio Armani

Is this a good time to open your salon? Our answer is, "Yes," as long as you find the right location and negotiate a great commercial lease. Since the downturn of the economy, we have seen a huge decrease in commercial shopping center occupancy. Some centers are only 50 percent filled with tenants. Landlords are looking for any opportunity to lease their location and they are giving incredible deals to fill their growing empty spaces.

This creates a huge opportunity that would normally cost you much more. The key is to know what to look for and what questions to ask. Realize that your rent will be one of the largest fixed expenses you have every month.

The importance of negotiating this lease agreement will help you with your budget and financial outlook. Any miscalculations made on the negotiating of this lease will be with you the entire term of the lease. That problem will be very costly and, unfortunately, does not go away once you sign the agreement.

When you are looking for a location for your salon, most are available for lease only, not to own or buy. But, before you agree to the basic terms of the commercial lease that the landlord hands you, you should realize that there is plenty of leeway in commercial leases for negotiations. Here are the most common facts that will assist you when negotiating your lease and will enable you to get the best deal possible.

- Analyze all costs associated with the potential space (construction, air conditioning, handicap-access bathrooms)
- Is it a triple net or gross lease? Triple net means there are added expenses such as maintenance and property taxes. Gross is a total lease amount with no add-ons.

- City impact fees (example: one-time water hookup with the city)
- Any restriction on services?
- Deposits and down payments
- Free rent

Basic Lease Cost

The first item of business you and your landlord will need to discuss is how much you will pay to rent the space. Usually, your monthly rent will be determined based on the square footage of the space, which is calculated at a per square foot cost. If you take the width and the length, multiply it by the dollars per square feet, and then divide it by 12, that will give you your base monthly rent.

Additional Costs

Sometimes you will have additional costs to figure into your monthly rent expense, called CAM (common area maintenance) or triple net. It is often an addition to the monthly rent or an annual assessment per tenant. The CAM costs are added up as follows: The CAM includes the maintenance of any common areas, like walkways, landscaped places, parking lots, and, in some cases, restrooms.

It is common for the landlord to concede and include CAM charges in the rent price of your commercial lease if negotiated correctly. Getting the most of your leased space is often determined by the market conditions of your location.

Below are some additional CAM expenses to look for when negotiating your lease:

- Property tax
- Snow removal, lawn maintenance, landscaping
- Repairs and maintenance to driveways, sidewalks, or parking lots
- Utilities (electric, gas, sewer, and water)
- Refuse collection
- Security
- Insurance—prorated among tenants
- Structural and roof repairs
- Mechanical system repairs and replacements (such as heating and A/C maintenance and replacement)

> **NOTE**
>
> It is wise not to sign a lease until you are certain that your financing is secure. Otherwise, you may find yourself responsible for lease payments using your own money while you wait for a loan to come through.

Repairs & Improvements

These are a critical part in your lease negotiations. The build-out in a salon can be very expensive. Ideally, if the previous tenant was also a salon, changes could be minimal.

Three important factors to look for:

- The amount of electricity coming into the location
- The size of the air conditioner and heating unit
- Handicap-access bathroom requirements

Plumbing, electric, handicap-access bathrooms, lighting, flooring, and painting are all part of the move-in process. Be very careful when the landlord says "take it as-is." That means you will pay for all repairs and upgrades. If you can do these repairs or improvements yourself, you may be able to do them inexpensively. But, be careful! You will need to meet code requirements for any changes.

However, in most cases, the landlord will want a licensed contractor to do the work. Some landlords are willing to absorb the cost of reasonable upgrades since you are improving their property.

Financing Your Construction Costs

Obtaining financing from your landlord may be the easiest and the most overlooked method of getting financing. Many landlords have already built money into their financial projections that they will use to attract new tenants. These tenant improvement allowances can range from $5 to $25 per square foot.

The new tenant can use the landlord's contractors to build-out the space necessary for the salon. The landlord will pay the contractor and reimburse you the monies spent for all the build-out once you provide them with documentation. The required documentation which usually includes lien waivers from all contractors/subcontractors and copies of Notice of Occupancy permits from the city/county. Negotiate the tenant improvements upfront and right into the lease.

Signing Your Life Away—Personal Guaranty

Definition:

- A guarantee that the primary owner will assume personal responsibility for repayment of the loan, should the company not repay the loan.

    www.businesstown.com/finance/money-glossary.asp

- An agreement to make oneself liable or responsible to another for the payment of a debt, default, or performance of a duty by a third party.

www.crfonline.org/orc/glossary/p.html

- The provision in a lease naming a guarantor who is held personally responsible for the payment of all the amounts for rent and additional rent and other terms as set out in the lease.

www.gtacommercialrealestate.com/resources.asp

How can you avoid giving a personal guaranty when signing a lease? For almost all new businesses, landlords will want you to sign personally. We recommend signing as a limited liability entity such as a corporation, limited liability, or limited partnership. Try to avoid signing a personal guarantee at all costs.

Tenants should not grant the landlord a security deposit with an interest in the salon furnishings, inventory, and trade fixtures. A security deposit of first and last month's rent payment should suffice.

Buyout Clause

The tenant should negotiate, upfront, a buyout clause in the lease negotiations. Doing so will allow the tenant of a new business to get out of the lease should the business fail. If the tenant should desire to terminate the lease, the "buyout" clause would be in place. The buyout should provide that the tenant can pay a specific amount of rent, usually from three to six months, to terminate the lease.

Free Rent

It's important in the first year to negotiate a very low rent to allow you to turn a profit quickly or utilize your dollars elsewhere, such as in advertising and marketing. You might be able to negotiate six months free rent in the beginning or half rent. There are so many ways to be creative.

Free rent can be very helpful in the beginning stages of setting up your business—it doesn't matter whether you are opening your first salon, relocating your current salon, or opening another location. Free rent is free rent and can help offset the costs of your business venture.

Here are some reasons why free rent is so important:

- Construction time, including permits, takes 3-4 months; free rent during this building process (no revenue at this point)
- Promoting the salon during construction
- Using available money for advertising and marketing
- Bringing staff onto payroll as the salon is being built
- Loss of your existing employment while building your new business

Details of Your Commercial Lease Negotiations

Check off the questions below as you get answers.

○ Did you discuss what signage will be acceptable?

○ What happens if you need to relocate?

○ What if an employee wants to buy your business? Can they take over the lease?

○ What happens if you outgrow your space?

○ What happens if you want to downsize?

○ What happens if you go out of business?

Final Steps—Legal Advice

As a final precaution, take the lease to an attorney who specializes in lease agreements. You can never be too careful about signing a commercial lease. Your lawyer will raise any red flags, answer your questions, and explain exactly what you are signing.

Salon Owner/Operators Discuss the Good, the Bad, & the Ugly

Harry Holmann, Creative Hair

"I had an attorney dissect every part of the lease before I would sign anything. No matter how many times I read the lease, my attorney was able to pick up some very important things that I missed that would have cost me a ton of money."

CHAPTER 6

Your Legal & Financial Team

"I have no use for bodyguards, but I have very specific use for a highly trained accountant."

—Elvis Presley

Sometimes, we come across salon owners who tried to research and manage all the legal and financial situations on their own. We are here to tell you that "going it alone" can be a costly mistake. While educating yourself on the legal and financial aspects of business and salon ownership is always a good idea, don't undervalue or disregard the importance of a good legal and financial team. Educating yourself will make it easier to talk to and understand your lawyer, accountant, and bookkeeper. We are firm believers in learning as much as you can about operating your business. However, from a legal and financial standpoint, each business property lease and business model is different and having the skilled expertise of your lawyer or accountant looking at the finer details will pay off—big time.

Do what you do best—your forte is hair and beauty!

When you put together your legal and financial team, you will want to find professionals who represent small business owners or even other salon owners. Lawyers and accountants can be costly, but paying for their services and expertise will save you from the financial losses you could face from poorly negotiated lease agreements, unnecessary lawsuits, late or incorrect tax payments, etc.

Just like everything else in this business venture, you will need to do your research to find the good ones—the ones who will do their best for you. When you need them, you want to know they are there for you and that they understand your business needs! In this chapter, you will find helpful tips about hiring the right lawyer, accountant, and bookkeeper for your business.

Hiring a Lawyer

Having a good business lawyer is essential in negotiating the best lease and properly setting up your business entity. Many aspects of business require legal advice. Once your business is open, you may have issues with other tenants, your landlord, your clients, or your employees that will require the assistance of a lawyer. When a legal problem arises, not having legal representation can put you in a costly position—a position that could have been easily avoided had you secured a lawyer early on in your business venture.

Hiring an attorney and forming a solid business relationship with him or her, can save you money and mitigate risk throughout the course of owning and operating your business.

Here are some examples of why you need an attorney:
- Signing your business property lease
- Negotiating with the landlord
- Forming your business structure
- Closing on the purchase of real estate
- Closing on the purchase of an existing salon
- Litigating any lawsuits

However, if you run into a small problem and you feel it can be handled without the advice of a lawyer, then you can find the right forms or information on legal portals such as AllLaw, found at alllaw.com.

The solution is to have open communication with a lawyer who will be ready to work with you quickly if a situation arises. Get legal advice if you have any questions that will cost you money, whether the legal issue is with your business or personal.

What Kind of Lawyer Do You Need?

Lawyers typically specialize in one type of law or another. You are best off finding a business lawyer who specializes in small businesses. However, a general practice lawyer can handle a wide range of legal matters and may be suited to your business needs.

If a legal matter involves a specialized kind of law like bankruptcy, litigation, taxation, or patent laws, then you need to contact a specialist. Make sure to ask your lawyer whether he or she specializes in a type of law before you decide to hire him or her.

Where Do You Find a Lawyer?

The best way to find a lawyer is through a friend, business acquaintance, or a client referral. You can also use an online directory where information is available about lawyers at their websites. Your state's bar association will also have a referral service that can help put you in touch with a lawyer that best suits your needs. We still say word of mouth and a good old-fashioned phone book are the best methods of finding a lawyer.

Find at least three prospective lawyers. Next, make an appointment and interview the lawyer. Ask questions pertaining to your business needs. The lawyer's answers will give you an indication about whether this lawyer is suitable for you and your business.

Questions to Ask a Prospective Lawyer

Check off the questions below as you ask them.

- ◯ What type of law do you specialize in?
- ◯ Do you have any salon owners for clients?
- ◯ What is your experience with negotiating a lease?
- ◯ What are the top three things you look to do for a business owner when negotiating a lease?
- ◯ What experience do you have with employment law?
- ◯ What are your legal fees—are your fees hourly or do you charge a flat rate?
- ◯ Are paralegals or associates available to handle routine matters at lower rates?
- ◯ How long have you been a lawyer and what has been your area of focus?
- ◯ Do you actively write articles or present at seminars for other professionals?
- ◯ What if a matter arises that is outside of your area of expertise?
- ◯ What is your availability to take on new clients and how responsive are you?

How Much Do Lawyers Charge?

Lawyers' fees can sometimes be very expensive. It all depends on what type of legal advice they are giving; and, most importantly, how much time they are spending on your needs. There are many different types of fee arrangements. Most lawyers charge hourly fees. Their fees are calculated by multiplying the amount of hours they spend on your case by an hourly rate.

If a lawyer is reviewing your real estate lease, he may charge you a preset amount or fixed fee. If he or she is filing your articles of incorporation for your new business, he may also charge you a fixed fee. You should always ask a potential lawyer to explain their fees and billing practices. Don't take things for granted. You might think that the attorney only took a few minutes to help you; and then, later, you receive a bill for a few thousand dollars.

Reading documents, especially your lease for your business, takes more than a few minutes for a lawyer to review. However, a lawyer can save you thousands over the term of your lease when they find and flag loopholes or clauses that are in the favor of your landlord.

Most lawyers require a retainer to get started. In the case of a real estate closing or filing articles of incorporation, the lawyer will send you a bill or you can pay them the day of closing. They usually will have a bill prepared and you will know the detailed breakdown of their fees before the closing.

You also have to remember that you are responsible for court fees, services, or any charges to the lawyer while representing you. This includes the time it takes your lawyer to get to and from the courthouse or legal meetings. Having a good lawyer at hand is one key to having a successful business.

Hiring an Accountant

Just like you need a lawyer to help with the legal matters of your business, you will need an accountant to advise you on the financial aspects of your business. Don't make the mistake of attempting this one on your own.

We tend to think of accountants when it comes to taxes, but there are many other services your accountant will provide. Whether you're deciding if you should incorporate your new business or trying to decide whether to buy or lease your salon equipment, a good accountant will be able to tell you how such decisions would affect your taxes and/or your businesses growth.

You need to make sure that you feel comfortable with the accountant you will be hiring. The accountant should be sincere and trustworthy. If you are clear about your requirements, then you will be able to choose the right accountant.

How to Find the Right Accountant

The easiest way to find a good accountant is by asking other business associates who they use for accounting services. You must ask them what type of services their accountant provides; and, most importantly, are they satisfied with the services the accountant offers? If you don't get any worthy referrals using this method, use the Internet to find accountants that are close to where you will be opening your salon. Close proximity to your accountant will make it easier and more manageable for communication and availability. Yes, you can learn QuickBooks; but, your time is better spent in other areas—like managing the salon and cutting hair.

The Face-to-Face Meeting

Face-to-face meetings are imperative because your accountant is someone you will see throughout the year and this person is going to get to know the most intimate details of your personal and business finances. They will also help you to mold your business for success. You are finding a long-term partner to advise you on the financial matters of your business. It's a big deal. You are establishing a lasting relationship that must be built on trust.

Questions to Ask a Prospective Accountant

Check off the questions below as you ask them.

- ◯ Are you a CPA? (Don't be afraid to ask him or her about their education.)
- ◯ Do you work with any other salons? If so, how will you avoid conflict?
- ◯ If you have worked with salons, what type of services did you offer?
- ◯ What type of salon software programs are you familiar with?
- ◯ Will you help grow my business or are you going to be more of a bookkeeper?
- ◯ Will you help me set up yearly tax planning? (They should be able to advise your business so it functions with peak tax efficiency.)
- ◯ Will you offer your personal finance advice? (A key to a good accountant is not just managing your business, but also managing your personal finances as well. Both business and personal finances, when managed correctly, are key to your success.)
- ◯ Does this accounting firm have the state-of-the-art technology and software needed to enable me to work and communicate with you efficiently? Describe it. (Technology has improved small business capabilities. Good communication is vital with your accountant, and the Internet has made that easy.)
- ◯ What organizations do you belong to?
- ◯ Are you affiliated with a local bank? (You may never know when you need a loan. There is an old saying: "It is not how much you know to be successful, but who you know." Don't look at your new accountant as just a bookkeeper; ask them if they have the ability to refer business to your new salon.)
- ◯ What type of business advice would you give me right now before I open that could help save me money? (Their answer to this question will give you a good idea if this person is right for you.)
- ◯ Why should I hire you? (The answer they give will paint a clear picture if they fit in your business plan.)

Finding a Bookkeeper

Your accountant will probably recommend that you also have a bookkeeper to help keep your finances organized and tracked in a timely manner. Having a bookkeeper on your financial team will help you to be better prepared for visits with your accountant and save you money in the long run.

You will find that the daily grind of opening the salon, running to the bank, credit card processing, scheduling staff, and dealing with all the new personalities is a lot to manage. Having someone else who is responsible for keeping your finances organized is essential.

Your bookkeeper should be required to:

- Keep track of checks and other income
- Process credit card balances
- Pay bills and reconcile the business checkbook
- Pay employees as well as file and pay federal and state payroll taxes
- Pay quarterly business taxes
- Keep track of receivables
- Keep track of inventories and commissions to your staff

When choosing your bookkeeper, it is important that you hire an individual who has the same business ethics on how to run your business YOUR WAY with their guidance.

> **Salon Owner/Operators Discuss the Good, the Bad, & the Ugly**

Dawn Brown Garrett

"My mistake was my choice of a business partner and attorney."

Nancy Williams, Raise Your Hair

"I tried to manage without an accountant and bookkeeper. I really have no experience in bookkeeping. Within six months of opening my salon, I was behind on my taxes. I hired an accountant that a client recommended and she saved my business. The best thing I ever did. I don't know what I would do without her."

Suzy Tryall, Noel's House of Color, Denver, CO

"I thought QuickBooks was my answer to hiring an accountant. I learned the hard way I should have stuck to what I do best......Hair!"

CHAPTER 7

Choosing a Business Structure

"Corporation: an ingenious device for obtaining profits without individual responsibility."

—Ambrose Bierce

New salon owners need to have an understanding and make a choice of how they want to legally set up their business. Even existing salon owners need to revisit their business structure because there are several choices when it comes to the types of legal organizational structure. The type of business structure you decide upon will affect how much you pay in taxes, the amount of paperwork your business is required to do, the personal liability you face, and your ability to borrow money. An accountant or a lawyer can assist you with the choice that would be best for you and the success of your business.

The business structure you choose will lay down the foundation you need to conduct a legal business enterprise and will also protect you in case you or one of your employees causes an accident and/or damages to one of your clients or your landlord's property. If a lawsuit arises from the accident, your home, business, and assets could be at risk if not properly protected. The legal structure you select should protect you in these cases. However, many first-time salon owners often overlook or ignore the ability to choose the business structure that will give them the greatest protection.

Sole Proprietorship

A sole proprietorship is the simplest and most straightforward form of business organization. It is easy to form and offers complete control to the owner. It is an unincorporated business owned entirely by one individual and does not require massive amounts of complicated tax forms.

A salon owner who operates with no other employees besides themselves usually chooses a sole proprietorship. This can be a home-based business or operated out of a retail commercial location. In general, the owner is also personally liable for all financial obligations and debts of the business.

Every sole proprietor is required to keep sufficient records to comply with federal tax requirements regarding business documents. They do not have taxes withheld from their business income; they will need to make quarterly estimated tax payments. These estimated payments include both income tax and self-employment taxes for Social Security and Medicare.

One advantage of the sole proprietorship is that additional expenses, such as office expenses, property taxes, utilities, and vehicle expenses may be deducted from the proprietor's income on their taxes.

The liability of a sole proprietorship is the full responsibility for any debt and liability and lawsuit that the company might incur. It means that the individual salon owner is held personally responsible for damages, problems, or adverse consequences resulting from the operation of the business.

Partnership

A partnership is the relationship existing between two or more persons who join each other to carry on a business with one goal—to earn a profit. Each person contributes money, property, labor, or skill and expects to share in the profits and losses of the business.

It is usually assumed, under most states' laws, that all partners will share control over the business equally. You can state in the partnership agreement which partners are responsible for the job description to which they agree. You may also want to establish voting rights based on the percentage of the initial investment or how the amount of work and hours will be distributed amongst each partner. Your agreement should spell all of this out prior to opening the salon.

In addition, you can specify in your partnership agreement how profits, losses, and salaries will be allocated among partners. It is also based on initial investment and time put into the business. If everyone is equal and puts in the same investment, this agreement becomes very easy.

A partnership agreement should also address the eventuality of a partner leaving the business, a partner who is no longer capable of working in the salon, the death of a partner, and the addition of new partners.

Partnership Taxation

Like a sole proprietorship, a partnership has one level of taxation. A partnership is a tax-reporting entity, not a tax-paying entity, which means that profits pass through the partnership to the owners and are divided in accordance with what was agreed to and specified in the partnership agreement. There are no restrictions on how profits are allocated among partners as long as there is economic reason. The partners are responsible for good bookkeeping, paying their tax obligation, Social Security, and Medicaid.

Liability

While there are many benefits of a partnership, one disadvantage is that the owners have unlimited personal liability for their own actions and the actions of their partners. In general, each partner in the salon is jointly liable for the partnership obligations. Joint liability means that the partners can be sued as a group. In some states, each partner can be held accountable for the damages from the wrongdoing of other partners and for the debts and obligations of the partnership.

Three rules for liability in a partnership are:

- Every partner is liable for his or her actions.
- Every partner is liable for the actions of the other partners.
- Every partner is liable for the actions of the employees of the business.

Corporation

There are many reasons to form a corporation to conduct business. Many entrepreneurs aren't comfortable remaining in a sole proprietorship and require a level of protection not afforded by a sole proprietorship. While some owners think incorporating is only for big companies, the most common form of a business now is to own and operate a business as a corporation.

A corporation is commonly referred to as a limited company or just "company."

Some of the main advantages of using a corporation to conduct business include the following:

- Limited Liability: The owners of the corporation are shareholders in the business and are not liable for the debts and obligations of the corporation. Creditors cannot hold the shareholders responsible for the debts of the corporation. If the company cannot pay its debt, the creditors cannot go after the shareholders personally. This is one of the main reasons people form a corporation.

- Ownership Easily Transferable: Ownership of a corporation is transferred easily by transferring the shares. It can be as simple as endorsing the back of the share certificate.

- Tax Advantages: If a corporation operates as a small business and has active income, then it can take advantages of small business deductions and pay income taxes at a substantially reduced rate. There can be a significant tax savings compared to doing business outside of a corporation. A corporation files a separate income tax return. If a shareholder is an employee, he pays income tax on his wages, and the corporation and the employee each pay one-half of the Social Security and Medicare taxes and the corporation can deduct half. A corporate shareholder only pays income tax for any dividends received.

- Raising Capital: It is easier to raise capital for a corporation than it is for a partnership or sole proprietor. Lenders are more willing to lend capital to a corporation.

Limited Liability/LLC

A limited liability corporation, also known as an LLC, is a relatively new legal business definition which was formed specifically to provide a host of benefits to new business owners not offered by other entities. Given all the benefits and flexibility to business owners, business people, lawyers, and accountants, now consider the limited liability corporation as the presumptive choice for new business.

Liability Benefits

One of the biggest benefits of an LLC is that all owners of a limited liability company are protected from being personally liable for the debts, obligations, and lawsuits of the LLC. The LLC benefit states that a member is not liable just because he or she is a member/owner of the LLC. There are guidelines that need to be followed by the principals and/or the members of the LLC so this protection is not lost.

Informal Decision Making

In an LLC, the owners determine the ownership structure, the right to the profits, voting rights, and any other aspect of relationships amongst members. An LLC does not require a board of directors, shareholder meetings, and other managerial formalities, which allow the owners to focus more on their business and less on the requirements and maintenance of corporate guidelines and mandates.

Flexible Tax Choices

The tax choices for an LLC are the second biggest benefit of an LLC for small business owners. The single-member LLC (owned by an individual) can take advantage of having simple sole proprietorship federal income taxation, but without the personal liability of the sole proprietorship.

What does that mean? As a salon owner, you are able to write off all the expenses of a home office, utilities, and car. Usually, you would normally not have the benefit of doing so. Both a single and multimember LLC can choose to be taxed as a corporation as well. The tax benefits of an LLC provide more choices than other legal entities.

When you finally do decide which legal structure is right for your business, it's important to choose the entity that gives you the most protection from personal liability with the best tax advantages for your specific situation.

Only a good numbers person can look at your current situation and long-term goals to give you the kind of sound objective counsel you need to make the best decision. A good CPA may cost you some upfront money; but, in the long run, it will be money well spent.

CHAPTER 8

Setting Up Your Business Checking Account

Opening a business checking account is one of the first of many things you will be doing when starting your new salon. It is a necessity for corporations and limited liability corporations (LLCs). The opening of a business account will eliminate the commingling of business and personal funds. Keeping business funds separate helps you keep track of transactions made in your business, maintain good records for tax time, and monitor the financial health of your business.

Many new and existing salons have three separate checking accounts. They use one for paying bills, another for payroll, and one for credit card processing. It is important that you choose a bank that is in close proximity to your salon or your home. Doing so will allow you to develop a personal relationship when you stop into your bank with deposits or any other issues you may have in the course of your daily business operation.

Business owners should research the different business accounts offered at various banking institutions to determine which business account best suits the needs of their salon business. You can open a business bank account through a bank or credit union. Many will allow you to start the account application process in person, by phone, or online. We feel that a one-on-one meeting with your new banker is the best way to establish a new business relationship with your bank. Your banker will be one of the most important people you do business with on a daily basis.

When trying to figure out what bank best suits your needs, it may pay to start with the financial institution where you currently have your personal account. Since you already have a relationship established, you can easily ask them what type of business programs they have.

Which Bank Is Right for You?

Check off items below as you consider your bank options.

- ○ Close proximity to work or home for convenience of making daily deposits
- ○ Free check writing
- ○ Lower business processing fees
- ○ Better interest rates on a loan based on the deposits you bring in daily
- ○ Free debit cards
- ○ Online banking and bill paying
- ○ Fee structure for all business transactions
- ○ Interest earned on daily monies in your business checking account
- ○ Business savings account
- ○ Willingness to consider giving you a loan for future growth or expansion
- ○ Understanding of the beauty industry (Do they have any salons as customers?)
- ○ Free ATM transactions
- ○ What type of balances do you have to maintain to keep your business checking account open? (Knowing this information when you open your account will help you avoid fees.)
- ○ Free business checks
- ○ Overdraft protection on your account
- ○ No fees for bounced checks

Once you have determined the bank that works best for your business, you will need to open your account. Check with your new banker in regards to what items they require when opening your account; each bank is different. Paperwork will depend upon your type of business ownership and what type of business accounts you want to open. Generally, you will need the following items:

EIN–Employer Identification Number

Every corporation, partnership, or LLC must present its Employer Identification Number to obtain a business bank account. Your EIN number is a nine-digit number used to identify the company for banking and taxation purposes. Your EIN number will show your legal name and the owners of the company and the shares they own. Sole proprietors who do not have an EIN will be required to use their Social Security Number to open a business checking account.

Articles of Incorporation

A new business needs to present its formation documents to establish a business account. Corporations (INCs) must present articles of incorporation, while Limited Liability Corporations (LLCs) must present articles of organization to open a business bank account. Partnership businesses must present a copy of the company's partnership agreement to verify the existence of the company.

Businesses that operate as a sole proprietorship will be required to submit the name filing or trade name certificate to the bank. Sole proprietors who have chosen to use the legal name of the business owner are not required to submit a trade name certificate. They may only need a business license when opening the new account.

Resolution

A resolution must be submitted to the bank to identify the individuals who are authorized to use the business bank account. The resolution should include the name, address, Social Security Number, and position of each person authorized to use the company's account. Sole proprietors do not require a resolution; usually the business owner is the only person authorized to use the account, unless a manager or bookkeeper is requested to do so. In a partnership, each partner may have equal access to use the company's business bank account.

Identification

The people identified in the corporate resolution must bring the appropriate identification to establish a business bank account. Driver's license, Social Security card, birth certificate, and/or passport will be necessary when you open the account.

Initial Deposit

Most banks require a small deposit to open a business account; but, a larger deposit is a smart move to avoid those unpleasant bank service charges. You can open a business account for only $25 at most banks around the country.

✓ CHECK IT OUT

Check off the items below as you obtain or gather them:

- ◯ EIN (Employer Identification Number)
- ◯ Articles of Incorporation
- ◯ Resolution
- ◯ Identification
- ◯ Initial Deposit

Salon Owner/Operators Discuss the Good, the Bad, & the Ugly

Stefanie G Salon

"I never opened a business checking account. The first year in business I ran all my business and household expenses through my personal checking account. Then I got a letter from the IRS. I went through the worst audit of my life. I had to explain every check I wrote and why. It took so much of my time. When it was over, I had to pay. My laziness cost me over $5000. Don't ever commingle business with personal."

CHAPTER 9

Licenses & Permits to Start Your Business

Starting your salon business is going to require a "To Do List" a mile long. Many tasks need to be completed before you even think about opening your doors for business, including adherence to state requirements. You will need to obtain a number of licenses and permits from federal, state, and local governments. Every city and state has different laws and requirements when starting a new business.

The process can sometimes be long and confusing. Start filling out the paperwork as soon as you can, expect delays, and provide all the information necessary to avoid any problems with the opening of your business. For the most part, the different requirements are all variations of a few basic elements. Keeping this in mind, we have listed below the different types of licenses and permits you may need to acquire prior to opening for business.

Business Operation License

When operating a salon and selling retail, you will be required to have a basic business operation license from the city or from the local county. The process for gaining a license will be different in each city or state, but will require an application fee, the name of the owner, name of the company, nature of the business, and where the owner plans to operate. Make sure your application is accepted and you meet all of their requirements. You will not be able to open your doors without this.

- Your state website has all state applications online
- Your local municipality has all local applications available

Certificate of Occupancy

Most local governments will require a Certificate of Occupancy, issued by the building department. The certificate is to ensure that you comply with applicable building codes and other laws, and indicates your building to be in a condition suitable for occupancy. The Certificate of Occupancy is also necessary to close on a mortgage if you constructed a building for your salon.

License to Sell Retail

Many states require you to have a license to sell different types of retail products. In the salon business, you will be selling mainly haircare products. Your town may not require any specific license for this.

Federal Employer Identification Number (EIN)

If the state in which you operate has state income tax, you will have to register and obtain an Employer Identification Number from your state Department of Revenue or Treasury Department. For more information, go to www.irs.gov.

Fire Department Permit

Most of the time, this permit is a town requirement and requires that an annual fee be paid. A fire safety person will come to your location before the salon opens to make sure you have met the fire department's safety requirements. The requirements are smoke detectors, proper fire exits and signage, and fire extinguishers.

Building Permits

If you plan on doing any extensive remodeling of the space you will occupy or make any changes, your town may require electrical or plumbing permits. The requirements and permits will always fall back on the occupant of the space, but your contractor should take care of these permits and make sure they are filed with the town, inspected, and met without any contingencies.

Cosmetology License

It is illegal to practice cosmetology or barbering without a valid license. It will be your responsibility as an owner to make sure you and your employees meet the state guidelines with continuing education to keep your license valid. The state will send an inspector to your salon to review each of your employees' licenses to make sure they are current and displayed visibly in the salon.

Check off the permits below as you obtain them.

○ Business Operation License

○ Certificate of Occupancy

○ License to Sell Retail

○ Federal Employer Identification Number (EIN)

○ Seller's Permit

○ Fire Department Permit

○ Building Permits

○ Cosmetology License

CHAPTER 10

Designing & Space-Planning Your Salon

"Great opportunity is related to great design; you rarely get one without the other."

—Giorgio Armani

Once you have picked your location and signed the lease, it's time to plan your space. In most shopping centers, a lot of the locations that are available are rectangular with the following dimensions:

- 20'x60' or 1200 square feet
- 20'x70' or 1400 square feet
- 30'x80' or 2400 square feet

In this chapter, we will dissect each zone, talk about the different types of furniture to use, and the ways to make each department efficient and esthetically pleasing.

When walking into your salon, the most important thing is the client's first impression or the "WOW" factor. The experience sets the tone in someone's mind about the salon. It is very important to give an excellent "first impression." Go back to Chapter 2 and look at what you wrote down and how you described your dream salon.

Reception or Front Desk

When the client initially walks into the front door, it is important that their eyes have a focal point on retail and a person to go to for immediate direction. So, it's critical to have the reception desk near the entrance to the salon. The desk should be both functional and pleasing to the eye, because that's one of the first things your client sees.

The receptionist must be ready to direct this customer and make them feel welcome. The reception or front desk area of the salon must look clean, organized, and professional.

The size of the desk is a big variable, depending on the size of the salon and the amount of staff. In a large salon, you might have a "check-in desk" for arriving clients and a separate "checkout desk" for making service payments and scheduling future appointments. Every salon location and setup is different. Most reception desks contain a place for one or two phones, a computer, a keyboard, a printer, and a writing shelf for the customer. When designing your desk, keep functional space in mind and make the size big enough to manage your operation properly.

When designing your salon, your reception desk must be designed to handle a lot of different functions, which include:

- Booking appointments
- Answering the phone
- Greeting customers
- Collecting payment for services rendered
- Selling other services and products
- Getting customers' email addresses or phone numbers for appointment reminders
- All accounting for daily work
- Updating client information

Retail Space

The opportunity for clients to learn about and make retail purchase decisions will occur three-to-four times while they are at your salon:

- When they check in
- When seated in the reception area
- While they are in the stylist's chair
- When they check out

It is very important to take advantage of these opportunities. Your retail displays are extremely important because selling retail brings in additional revenue to your business. Retail displays should be properly lit to showcase the products carried at your salon.

Unfortunately, most salon owners do not make retail a priority when designing and laying out their salon. This consideration has the most upside potential to create a retail revenue stream. We highly recommend utilizing a lot of space for retail. Call your local distributor to find out what type of retail units come with the product you will be purchasing. At a minimum, leave 5 feet of wall space in the reception area on both sides for wall displays. For freestanding displays, choose a style that fits into your design without compromising the flow of the salon. If you have the space, you should set up the zone like a "store" within your salon. It has a lot of appeal and gives the client the impression of a professional atmosphere.

Reception Seating

Above, we indicated standard sizes of a salon and for these sizes the retail/reception spot should be 200 to 300 square feet. So, if a salon is 20 feet wide, then your area is 10–15 feet deep. Doing so will give you room to put in an ample amount of retail space and seating for your clients.

Don't go overboard with a lot of reception seating. If you have an efficient front desk and timely service providers, people should not be sitting and waiting. Also, you want your clients to browse your retail zone. So, design the area for flow and interest in order to create more sales.

For an 8–10 station salon, we recommend 4–6 waiting chairs. It is a must to get individual chairs with arms. Steer away from couches or other options where clients are required to sit next to one another without any separation or barriers. It becomes an uncomfortable situation when your client is next to a "stranger" waiting for their appointment, especially on a couch. You want the client to feel at ease while they are waiting; having an individual chair for someone is the best approach for making them feel relaxed. Here is a typical design for the front of a salon:

Reception Seating Area

The Styling Area

The styling area is where your clients will spend the most time. Feeling comfortable in that space is very important to clients—they want privacy, roominess, and a place for their belongings. The minimum space for a wall station, from center-to-center of each station, is 4 feet 6 inches. It gives ample space for each stylist to work and does not waste any space. Salon owners have used as much as 6 feet for each station because of the station design. But, when considering revenue potential, adding another foot and a half to each station means that you miss out on being able to add two more stations, which is missed revenue opportunity. We recommend the biggest spread from center-to-center be no more than 5 feet. Any more than that is wasting space.

Freestanding Stations

In most cases, we recommend that freestanding stations are no wider than 36 inches and as narrow as possible. Most of the storage space needs to be located on the sides of the units with a small shelf in front, where the mirror is located. When discussing space planning, the unit is normally 36 inches wide and 30–36 inches deep. If you add chairs on each side, the unit takes up 12 feet of depth.

One thing that needs to be considered when discussing a freestanding unit is the walkway space around the unit where the stylist is working. This is usually a main traffic area. So, it is recommended that another 3 feet is added to each side for the flow. The overall depth of the station, including traffic, is 18 feet. It can change by the way you might angle the station, but you won't know until you space-plan the complete salon.

Be aware that you need to hook electrical to the freestanding station, which will either come from the floor or the ceiling. Either one can be expensive and must be researched while designing.

Potential added expenses for freestanding shampoo unit:

- Concrete floor, no basement: you will need to cut the concrete to run wiring
- Exposed wires from the ceiling: unattractive and may not get proper electrical approval
- Increased electrical panel expense: upgrading the service
- Additional lighting: need more light

Here are some general dimensions for laying out your styling stations:

Wall Mounted Styling Area

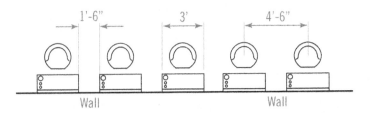

Freestanding Styling Area

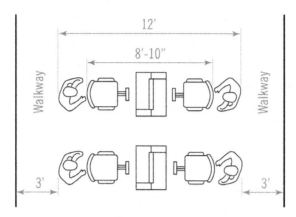

Styling Chair Design

1. Chair containing round or five-star bottom base: The overall dimensions are 24 inches by 24 inches around. Weight varies from chair to chair. A good quality chair usually has a weight of 60 pounds or more.

    a. Round base: more stability, with weight and diameter a factor. For cleaning, it is recommended that it be moveable because a ring develops from hair buildup around the base bottom.

    b. 5-star base: less stability and easier for a client to tip it over when putting weight on the footrest. Easier to clean by taking a hair blower and blowing out all the hair underneath the chair.

2. Chair containing a U-shaped or T-shaped footrest:

    a. U-shaped: this footrest is shaped like a U and has been in the industry for many years. Clients tend to trip over it when getting off the chair.

    b. T-shaped: this footrest was developed about 30 years ago, originally in Europe. A much better design for clients.

3. Styling chair with no footrest:

    Most of the time, you will see this chair in Europe or Asia, and they typically have a floor-mounted footrest for the client. They do not work for the U.S. market because in America the stylists like to turn the chairs to different positions, whereas in Europe, the stylist works around the chair. We do not recommend going with this style.

Cleaning & Maintenance

All your equipment needs to be cleaned and many people do not know what type of cleaner to use. Ninety-nine percent of all chairs manufactured these days are made of vinyl, which is a soft, expandable plastic material. Many chairs have hairspray buildup and owners do not know how to clean it. The best product is mineral spirits, which has an oil base and does not dry up the material like ammonia-based cleaning products. Leave the mineral spirits on for 5 minutes. Then, wipe the vinyl clean. For the base bottom and footrest, use a chrome polish product.

Shampoo Area

The shampoo area is no longer stuck in the back. Many salons make it an attractive, visible zone with the introduction of freestanding shampoo units that give the salon a dramatic look. This part of the salon is now considered a profit center for the salon, showcasing products that clients can buy.

Sink Guideline

# of stations	# of sinks
1	1
2-5	2
6-9	3
10-13	4
14-18	5

These guidelines do not include the color department sinks. You should use the same formula for calculating the amount of sinks if you have a color department.

Wall Sinks

Space-planning a shampoo zone for a wall sink usually has a rule of thumb: each sink takes up 4 feet of space; so, if you have three sinks, it will take up 12 feet of wall space. You can go a little smaller, but you should be very careful with spacing for wall sinks. Each sink is about 2 feet wide with 2 feet in between; anything less than that and your shampoo persons and stylists will find it difficult to get in between the shampoo sinks without bumping into the next sink.

Freestanding Backwash Shampoo Sinks

When space-planning for freestanding backwash sink units, the size is approximately 2 feet wide by 4 feet long, without a footrest. These units are usually spaced on center 30 inches apart from the center of each drain. Doing so gives 6-inches of space in between sinks. There are many ways to design how these sinks are situated, but you always need at least 30 inches of clearance behind them for the shampoo person to wash the client's hair.

You also must consider a cabinet behind the sinks for shampoos, conditioners, and towels. The rule of thumb is that a freestanding unit is to be at least 54 inches from the wall to give room for the shampoo person and a cabinet. You can also design the shampoo units to have a gap in between so you can shampoo from the side as well. The plumbing needs to be 48 inches on center.

> **NOTE**
>
> When purchasing freestanding units, be aware of the type of fittings that are supplied for hookup. Many of the fixtures are metric and do not fit easily to American pipe fittings. You will have to get adapters and it will be a time-consuming, aggravating project.

For the freestanding sinks, usually the floor needs to be cut (expensive) for waste and waterline installation. For most wall-hung sinks, the waste and waterlines can be installed in the wall and cutting the floor is unnecessary. Each location is different and we recommend you review this with your architect for the most cost-effective approach.

If you have a location with a basement, then cutting the floor is not an issue and it is very easy to move pipes and put the sinks where you desire. You will have to insulate the hot water lines in the basement because they are usually exposed. They will lose hot water temperature fast, especially in the winter.

Please refer to the diagrams below for reference for the different design layouts:

Wall Mount Shampoo Area

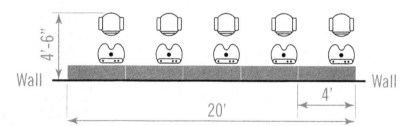

Free Standing Shampoo Area

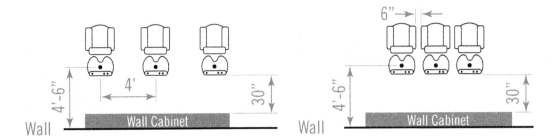

So, as you can see from the illustrations, there are three different ways to design your shampoo area. Be sure that you are comfortable with the design you pick.

Pedicure Unit

Now, it's time to talk about the pedicure zone. Can you believe over 40 companies manufacture all the different types of pedicure units? It can be very confusing. So, we will break down each type for you to decide.

Option 1: Chair With a Separate Footbath

It is the most basic style and the footbath ranges from $30 to $100, depending on the functions. The water must be filled and emptied by the pedicurist for each service. No plumbing is required and the "plastic" footbath needs to be sanitized after each use.

Option 2: Chair With a Separate Footbath and a Built-in Pump

This unit is portable and can be stored in a closet and taken out for a single use. After use, the unit needs to be brought (on wheels) over to a sink or toilet to discharge the dirty water, which is done by the pump in the unit. The price range for this type of unit is $775–$1100.

Option 3: Pedicure Unit Built Like a "Shoeshine" Bench

These do look very good and have a nice, cozy appeal. They can be built three different ways:

   a. Least expensive: unit with a portable footbath (described in #1)

   b. Unit with a built-in, flush-mounted. sink (kitchen style) which gives the pedicurist water for filling and draining.

   c. Unit with a whirlpool sink which looks like a kitchen sink, but contains the whirlpool capability with pumps built-in underneath the unit.

All of these built-in units look great and usually match the rest of the salon in the exact color. But, they all have the same common problem—the unit has no height adjustments.

The benches are designed to sit at a certain height. Many companies design the bench for an average person who is 5'6" tall. Let's say you have a male client that is 6'4" tall. When they sit in the unit, their knees are up to their chest! A woman who is 4'11" will need to slide down just to reach the bowl. Usually, pillows need to be propped for that person and the pedicure becomes an uncomfortable experience.

Some of these units come with nice options; but the bottom line is, if they have no height adjustment, they will not work well for all of your clients. Another possible issue is that these units are made of wood—most of them are plywood—but if water splashes on the surface and it's not sealed properly, the wood will swell or the Formica will delaminate over time. The price range for these units start at $800 for the base model and can go up to $4000 for all the bells and whistles.

Option 4:

Pedicure Unit With a Piped Whirlpool System

This type of unit has been in the industry for a long time. What we mean by "piped" is that tubes are running inside the unit and water gets pushed through the pipes by a motor, then the water is blown through jets that create a whirlpool action.

Over the last ten years, states have outlawed this type of unit. The reason is that after you use the unit, a small amount of water is left in the tubes inside of the unit. There is no way to sanitize the unit completely by flushing the system. If the unit is not used, the small amount of water left in the pipes builds bacteria, a natural process. Once the unit gets used again, bacteria may affect the client and create a rash or open sores. There are documented cases of this and we do not recommend this style unit. If you do buy this system, carry good insurance!! The unit ranges from $1300–$2000.

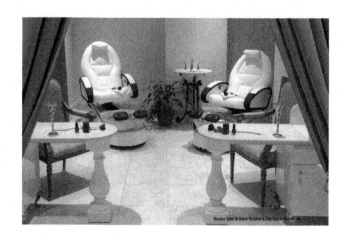

Option 5:

Pedicure Unit With a "Pipeless" Whirlpool System

A "pipeless" pedicure unit has all the same functions as the "piped" unit except it has no pipes. It contains a motor that is built behind a fan and it is mounted inside the tub that is covered by a plate. The plate protects you from any injury. The motor turns the fan, which creates a whirlpool, and after use, you take the cover off and sanitize it so there is no issue of bacteria. There are many types of units and the price range begins at $1800 and goes up to $12,000. My recommendation is that you buy this item from an established dealer. With a lot of these units, you have problems, regardless of brand, quality, or cost. You want to choose a reputable company so that you can count on them to still be in business when a problem arises with the unit.

Below is a typical pedicure layout.

3 Unit Pedicure Spa Room

Manicure Area

Now that we have finished the pedicure zone, we should talk about the manicure or nail department. What we have found in our experience is that most commissioned "nail techs" make on average about 70 percent commission. Once you buy supplies and handle all of the appointments, they are lucky to make 10 percent. Salons have manicurists as a service for their clients so that they come to their salon for more services, stay at their salon longer, and create more loyalty.

Our suggestion is that you rent the nail zone out and let them buy their own supplies. If you compare the numbers, you will make more money renting this department out with a lot fewer headaches. On the next page is a diagram to space-plan the zone. The normal size of a table is 48 inches long by 18 inches wide. The height of the table should be 30 inches.

We suggest that manicure tables be positioned against a wall and spaced 6 feet apart. That gives enough room for the client and nail tech to be comfortable.

Typical Manicure Area

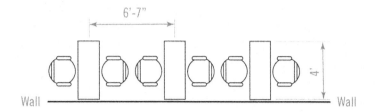

Color Department

The color department is where you "show me the money!" It is the most profitable department in a salon. It can be designed several different ways.

New Trend: The Color Lab or Bar—A unit built next to the color department in the open for the stylist to mix and prepare the color treatment for the client. It is visible for all to see and engages clients to feel part of the process and not alone. With this latest trend, you would have a dining-room style table with hydraulic styling chairs based around it and the colorist just brings a trolley over to work on the client.

This set up creates a more comfortable environment and clients are not as embarrassed as they used to be about having foils on their heads. All the color mixing is done at a "color lab or bar" as shown below. In the past, all mixing was done back in the dispensary. Now, salons mix the colors in front of their clients for client engagement. Colorists and stylists also feel more in touch and have better contact with their clients. For space-planning purposes, use the styling zone diagrams as your format.

Styles of Color Labs:

- Stainless steel
- Upper cabinet built with slots for color tube separation
- Sink for water capability
- Storage for all bowls and brushes
- Sizes range from 4–12 feet in length

Dispensary

Your dispensary is a necessary part of your salon. The diagram that follows illustrates a typical dispensary area. We have found that a dispensary measuring 13' x 14' (as shown) is suitable for most salons. Within this space, plan for a washer, dryer, hot water heater, sink, refrigerator, and an eating area. You may want to consider adding lockers for staff so they have a place to store personal items. You can purchase preassembled lockers from Sandusky Cabinets online at www.sanduskycabinets.com.

Typical Dispensary Area

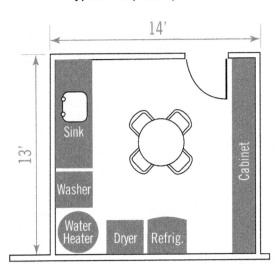

Each salon design is different and some cannot support such a spacious zone as the one above.

Hair Dryers With Chairs

The size of a typical dryer chair is 24 inches wide by 36 inches long. The weight is approximately 60 pounds with the dryer included. When space planning, please make sure that you have ample electrical outlets for power. Each dryer draws 9.8 amps at maximum use; we recommend you have access to a 20 amp plug. A four-dryer area needs 10 feet of space and about 48 inches of depth, not including walk-by traffic.

The amount of dryers that you should carry is based on the clientele and services you supply.

- Surrounded by retirement communities: recommend 1 dryer per 2 styling chairs

- Progressive coloring salon: recommend 1 dryer per 4 styling chairs

NOTE
A dryer on wheels can be useful for overflow.

Facial/Massage Area

The last department to talk about is the facial/massage area you might put into your salon. Following is a typical design for a three-room design. Two of the rooms are for facials and the other is for massage. A shower can be added but considering the cost involved, it is like adding another bathroom.

Typical Facial / Massage Area

9'-8"

8'-6"   8'-6"   8'-4"

Salon Owner/Operators Discuss the Good, the Bad, & the Ugly

Kayte G., House of Style

"My first salon I designed myself. I had no experience and wanted to do things my way. The mistakes I made cost me in the long run. I had stylists who wanted to join my team, but I did not have enough space. If I would have laid it out better, I would have had the room for growth. Use a salon professional or architect who has designed salons. It may cost you a few dollars, but you will be better off with the outcome! Once you design it, you are stuck with it for a long time. Make sure you are happy and it works for you and your team."

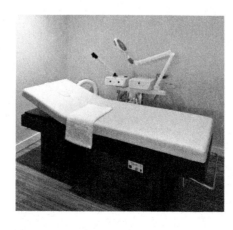

CHAPTER 11

Pricing Your Salon Furniture & Equipment

"A budget tells us what we can't afford, but doesn't keep us from buying it."

—William Feather

How to Choose the Right Furniture & Equipment for Your Salon

How exciting! It's time to place the furniture and equipment order for your new salon or for your salon remodeling project. When shopping for salon furniture and equipment, there are many things to consider. Selecting the appropriate furniture can add to your salon's business and growth. The kind of furniture and equipment you choose determines the environment of your business. The style and look you choose will determine what types of clients your salon will draw. Quality salon furniture and equipment, placed in an inviting atmosphere, is the perfect complement to a great salon environment.

Have you ever redesigned a space in your home? You probably started with some inspiration. Whether it was something you saw in a magazine or whether your design centered on a unique piece of pottery or art, you had something that helped you keep your choices aligned with your inspiration. Designing your salon space and choosing your furniture and equipment is exactly the same type of experience. You'll be amazed–and possibly overwhelmed–by all the choices. So, you need to have a firm grasp on your brand, the clientele that you want to attract, and the experience that you are trying to create.

When choosing furniture and equipment, you should consider working with a designer who specializes in salon layouts. You may also want to have someone with you who shares your vision and can give you feedback. This will be helpful as the salon designer presents different options that meet your budget and design vision. A suitable salon designer should be able to make the design and purchasing experience simple, exciting, and memorable.

You'll have to decide on styles, sizes, colors, laminates, wood, metal, stained, painted, or natural finishes. Seating can be leather, vinyl, a beautiful fabric, and more. Once again, your salon designer should be able to guide you through making the right decision and help you choose a style and design that you will love. Keep in mind that the fabrics and colors you choose must be durable. They will get wet and most likely get color on them.

The furniture and equipment manufacturers and/or distributors will be able to furnish you with catalogs, swatches, and color samples of their products. They will also walk you through the different sizes and shapes of the furniture and equipment. They will be able to discuss competitive pricing, customer service, warranty, and repair policies.

The popularity of the Internet has made it very easy for the salon owner to shop online with the click of a button. The Internet is your "friend" when seeking affordable furniture and equipment. It also gives you the ability to build a budget based on a couple of different looks that you might want to create.

If budget is a concern, the Internet may be the best bet for both your furniture and equipment purchases. There are pros and cons when shopping for salon furniture and equipment online. It's very easy to return a shirt or blouse when you buy it online. If the color, fit, or quality isn't what you expected, you can stick it in a box and send it back through the mail. It is difficult to send back a styling chair, shampoo sink/bowl, or workstation. If you don't like it or you feel the quality will not hold up in your salon, then you are looking at expensive return shipment fees.

Furniture & Equipment Checklist

When ordering your salon furniture and equipment, did you remember to:

- ○ Choose a durable laminate for your workstations and dispensary area?
- ○ Choose a styling chair that is practical for your customers?
- ○ Choose a front desk that not only looks good in your reception area, but gives the front desk person the space needed to best serve your clients? (Remember, your front desk is the focal point of the salon.)
- ○ Design a retail unit for display and overstock?
- ○ Allow adequate space for your retail area?
- ○ Design a wet- and dry-towel storage area to meet state board standards?
- ○ Choose a shampoo backwash unit that fits in your space and allows staff access to customers?
- ○ Allow adequate space for a dispensary or color storage?
- ○ Explore the option of a color lab?
- ○ Look at what you need in your salon office and backroom?

Furniture & Equipment Budget/Pricing

We have put together different furniture and equipment budgets based on three different types of salons: budget, mid-range, and high-end. This should give you the formula you need to pick the furniture and equipment that best suits your budget and style.

Budget Style Salon—Furniture & Equipment Pricing Breakdown (Example)

The table below contains pricing that is possible. However, products at this price point may not hold up or withstand the constant use you can expect at a busy salon. Although you may able to find these products through various outlets, we suggest that you purchase at the next pricing structure.

	Per Unit	4-Station	6-Station	8-Station
Styling chair	$175.00	$700.00	$1,050.00	$1,400.00
Dryer chair	$350.00	$1,400.00	$1,400.00	$1,400.00
Sink	$175.00	$350.00	$525.00	$700.00
Shampoo chair	$125.00	$250.00	$375.00	$500.00
Reception desk	$400.00	$400.00	$400.00	$600.00
Retail unit	$250.00	$250.00	$250.00	$500.00
Reception chair	$80.00	$320.00	$320.00	$480.00
Nail table	$140.00	$280.00	$280.00	$280.00
Styling station	$150.00	$600.00	$900.00	$1,200.00
Mirror	$75.00	$300.00	$450.00	$600.00
Pedicure unit	$600.00	$600.00	$600.00	$1,200.00
Stool	$75.00	$225.00	$225.00	$300.00
Shampoo cabinet	$300.00	$600.00	$900.00	$1,200.00
Color trolley	$80.00	$320.00	$480.00	$640.00
Shipping		$1,500.00	$2,200.00	$3,000.00
	TOTALS	$8,095.00	$10,355.00	$14,000.00

NOTES:

DRYER: for a 6- and 8-station salon, only 4 dryers are usually needed.

SINK: for a 6-station salon, 3 sinks; for an 8-station salon, 4 sinks.

RECEPTION DESK: for the 8-station salon, a larger desk is needed.

RETAIL UNIT: for an 8-station salon, a second retail unit is recommended.

RECEPTION CHAIR: for an 8-station salon, 6 chairs are recommended.

PEDICURE UNIT: a second unit is recommended for an 8-station setup.

STOOL: a 4th stool is recommended for the additional pedicure unit.

Other items, such as makeup, skincare, and massage, are not included in this budget. Most of the budget style salons do not have these services. Following is a breakdown if you decide to add this to your budget.

Additional Service Furniture & Equipment (Optional)	
Makeup station	$400.00
Makeup chair	$200.00
Facial table	$400.00
Multifunction facial unit	$700.00
TOTALS	$1,700.00

Mid-Range Style Salon–Furniture & Equipment Pricing Breakdown (Example)

	Per Unit	4-Station	6-Station	8-Station
Styling chair	$400.00	$1,600.00	$2,400.00	$3,200.00
Dryer chair	$600.00	$2,400.00	$2,400.00	$2,400.00
Sink & chair combined	$700.00	$1,400.00	$1,400.00	$2,100.00
Reception desk	$1,000.00	$1,000.00	$1,500.00	$2,000.00
Retail unit	$900.00	$900.00	$900.00	$1,800.00
Reception chair	$200.00	$800.00	$800.00	$1,200.00
Nail table	$400.00	$800.00	$800.00	$800.00
Styling station	$500.00	$2,000.00	$3,000.00	$4,000.00
Mirror	$150.00	$600.00	$900.00	$1,200.00
Pedicure unit	$2,500.00	$2,500.00	$2,500.00	$5,000.00
Stool	$150.00	$300.00	$300.00	$450.00
Shampoo cabinet	$600.00	$1,200.00	$1,200.00	$1,800.00
Color trolley	$150.00	$600.00	$900.00	$1,200.00
Shipping		$2,000.00	$2,600.00	$3,500.00
TOTALS		$18,100.00	$21,600.00	$30,650.00

	Per Unit	4-Station	6-Station	8-Station
NOTES:				
DRYER: for a 6- and 8-station salon, only 4 dryers are usually needed.				
SINK: for a 6-station salon, 3 sinks; for an 8-station salon, 4 sinks.				
RECEPTION DESK: for the 8-station salon, a larger desk is needed.				
RETAIL UNIT: for an 8-station salon, a second retail unit is recommended.				
RECEPTION CHAIR: for an 8-station salon, 6 are recommended.				
PEDICURE UNIT: a second unit is recommended for an 8-station setup.				
STOOLS: a 4th stool is recommended for the additional pedicure unit.				

Additional Service Furniture & Equipment (Optional)	
Makeup station	$1,000.00
Makeup chair	$300.00
Facial table	$1,200.00
Multifunction facial unit	$1,500.00
TOTALS	$4,000.00

The next breakdown we are illustrating is for a high-end salon. We have added color stations and processor. We added other services that might be used. You can make your own spreadsheet and determine your own breakdown.

HIgh-End Style Salon–Furniture & Equipment Pricing Breakdown (Example)

	Per Unit	4-Station	6-Station	8-Station
Styling chair	$1,200.00	$4,800.00	$7,200.00	$9,600.00
Dryer chair	$1,000.00	$4,000.00	$4,000.00	$4,000.00
Sink and shampoo chair	$2,500.00	$5,000.00	$7,500.00	$10,000.00
Reception desk	$3,000.00	$3,000.00	$3,500.00	$4,000.00
Retail unit	$2,000.00	$2,000.00	$2,000.00	$4,000.00
Reception chair	$400.00	$1,600.00	$1,600.00	$2,400.00
Nail table	$800.00	$1,600.00	$1,600.00	$1,600.00
Styling station	$2,000.00	$8,000.00	$12,000.00	$16,000.00
Mirror	$300.00	$1,200.00	$1,800.00	$2,400.00
Pedicure unit	$5,000.00	$5,000.000	$10,000.00	$10,000.00
Stool	$300.00	$600.00	$600.00	$900.00

(Spreadsheet is continued on next page)

(Spreadsheet is continued from previous page)

	Per Unit	4-Station	6-Station	8-Station
Shampoo cabinet	$1,200.00	$2,400.00	$900.00	$1,200.00
Color trolley	$400.00	$320.00	$480.00	$640.00
Color lab	$8,000.00	$8,000.00	$8,000.00	$8,000.00
Color chairs (2)	$800.00	$1,600.00	$1,600.00	$1,600.00
Color stations (2)	$1,500.00	$3,000.00	$3,000.00	$3,000.00
Dispensary	$2,500.00	$2,500.00	$2,500.00	$3,000.00
Makeup unit	$2,500.00	$2,500.00	$2,500.00	$2,500.00
Makeup chair	$500.00	$500.00	$500.00	$500.00
Facial table	$3,500.00	$3,500.00	$3,500.00	$3,500.00
Multifunction facial unit	$2,500.00	$2,500.00	$2,500.00	$2,500.00
Microdermabrasion	$3,000.00	$3,000.00	$3,000.00	$3,000.00
Vichy shower	$4,000.00	$4,000.00	$4,000.00	$4,000.00
Hydrotherapy tub	$3,500.00	$3,500.00	$3,500.00	$3,500.00
Color processor	$2,200.00	$2,200.00	$2,200.00	$2,200.00
Shipping		$3,500.00	$4,000.00	$5,000.00
	TOTALS	$79,820.00	$93,980.00	$109,040.00

NOTES:

DRYER: for a 6- and 8-station salon, only 4 dryers are usually needed.

SINK: for a 6-station salon, 3 sinks; for an 8-station salon, 4 sinks.

RECEPTION DESK: for the 8-station salon, a larger desk is needed.

RETAIL: for an 8-station salon, a second retail unit is recommended.

RECEPTION CHAIR: for an 8-station salon, 6 are recommended.

PEDICURE UNIT: a second one is recommended for a high-end salon.

STOOL: a 4th stool for the additional pedicure unit.

**All of these prices can vary. These figures will give you some idea of how much each level of salon will cost. You can use these figures as a starting point.

Installation

Installation can get quite costly. Local installation by the salon furniture and equipment company you are using can cost $500–$1000 per day. However, the price can vary. Be ready to negotiate after the first quote because you might be able to get their rate down depending on how badly they want the work. You might have your own installer, but there will be a cost.

• Local installer average per-day charge: $300

- Local installation without truck delivery per day by salon furniture company: $750
- Out-of-town installation: $1500 per day

Again, these prices are an average and may vary depending on the complexity of the job, the area, or location of the work, and whether the installation occurs over a weekend or in the evening.

When setting up delivery of your salon equipment, did you:

○ Have the equipment delivery company set up an inside-the-salon delivery or a curb delivery? If they aren't delivering inside, you will need help.

○ Check to see if your new equipment will fit through the front or back door of your salon?

○ Line up your contractor, electrician, and plumber for the next day after the delivery? Usually equipment deliveries come in the afternoon. No need to have expensive help standing around waiting for a delivery.

○ Inform staff to prepare for delivery, help set up, and prepare for opening or grand reopening?

○ Inform garbage service that you will need additional removal of boxes and crates?

○ Notify customers that you will be closing for a remodel and installation of new equipment?

Salon Owner/Operators Discuss the Good, the Bad, & the Ugly

JT, Crazy Style Cuts

"When I opened my first salon, I bought chairs for less than $200. I didn't have a lot of money. The chairs looked good, but didn't last long because of the constant use. I now have better quality chairs and my customers seem happier. Remember, you get what you pay for."

Juliana's New Look Hair Salon

"I bought a lot of my furniture online. It looked good in the pictures, but wasn't exactly what I thought. Price was right, but should have done more homework before buying."

CHAPTER 12

Your Retail Zone

*"In designing and baiting a mousetrap with cheese, always
remember to leave room for the mouse."*

—Saki

Retailing is a business within your salon that will make you money. Why is the backbone of most salon businesses overlooked and usually thrown together at the end of a new or remodel project?

The reason: Salon owners may not realize that retailing is essential for their business' success and did not give this area the attention it deserved during the space-planning and design process for their salon. Most salon owners focus on the service side of their business because that's where most of their experience lies. After all, that's why you opened your salon, to provide salon services, right?

It's a common oversight. But, if you picked the right salon designer, they will have guided you and made sure that you planned your retail zone in the salon layout.

Make sure that you plan this space properly. Your retail department must fit into the concept and design of the salon and should not be overlooked when designing and furnishing the space you have chosen for your retail.

Salon design and layout is exhausting and it will take a significant amount of effort and time to plan it properly. Once it is set, you don't want to go back and make last minute changes to "squeeze in" a retail area. And, you definitely don't want to make changes once you hit the expensive construction phase of your project. By planning properly, you will have budgeted for the build-out of this zone. Your investment in this area will make it easier to showcase your retail products. This chapter will help you choose the right fixtures for your selected retail area. Like furnishings in your home, the goal is to make it comfortable and convenient for those who work there and for the people who visit. The furnishings and display areas you choose should make it easy for the customers to browse and buy the salon retail products you are selling.

The most effective way to choose what type of fixtures and layout you like is by visiting other salons in and around your neighborhood. Studying salons or other stores that sell products like those offered in your salon will give you some great ideas for the types of displays that you like and designs that fit your location, style, and clientele. Using other peoples' ideas and modifying them to make them a natural fit for your space is an effective way to come up with exactly what you need to be successful in retail. Make sure you visit on a busy Saturday when salons and stores are busier. Then, you can see how the traffic flows in and out of the salon and around the retail areas.

Fine-Tune Your Plan

Your retail layout isn't ready until you can visualize it from your customers' perspective. In our experience, the most effective way to lay out a salon retail zone is by using empty boxes. The boxes should be placed where you are thinking about putting your display cases or shelving. Doing so will allow you to try all variations of your retail layout. This method should give you a perfect image of how things will look when you are ready to get your actual furniture and equipment. Invite some of your friends and families to fill the space so that you can see how the traffic will flow with your setup. Remember, once fixtures are put into place, they are not easy to move.

When laying out your retail zone, did you remember:

○ Space for clients to easily walk around

○ Storage and room for restocking

○ Critical space from fire exit or front door

○ Visual from salon or windows

○ Not to block windows

Selecting Primary Fixtures

We can't emphasize enough the importance of your retail area. L'Oreal has created a brand of retail display cases that emphasize space efficiency and provide a sleek, beautiful look to enhance any salon.

If your product supplier does not offer a branded option for retail display, then you will need to work with your salon designer. They can help you sort through the different looks and options for every budget and tailor something just for you.

The primary fixtures that you choose can be mixed and matched and some can be easily moved and placed in different locations. The type you choose should depend on what fits into your salon style, brand, and budget. Below, you will find a list of the most common fixtures found in salons around the world.

Bookcases

Most bookcases come in a variety of sizes and are very strong. A good quality bookcase will hold up, even with daily use. They usually are 7 feet tall and are 36 to 48 inches wide. We have seen salons stack these if they have the room, which is very effective. Most come with storage underneath. These units are made out of veneer products and come in a variety of colors.

Gondolas

Commonly referred to as islands, gondolas are open-ended display units with shelves on two or four sides. The most common size is 54 inches high, 48 inches wide and 36 inches deep. We have seen them with built-in storage units which makes it easy for restocking your retail products.

These units are becoming very popular in salons around the country. They provide a very comfortable approach to display and browse products. Keep in mind; you must have the appropriate room for the gondola units.

Pegboards

A long-standing retail display option, pegboards are the easiest and most cost-effective way to display your retail products. Pegboards are boards mounted on walls and frames with rows of holes in them to accept display pegs for your shelving.

We have seen these units in salon and retail stores around the world. If you are looking for a quick fix for space, this is it. If you are looking for a high-end look, this is not what you should use. Pegboards are efficient and work, but give a low-budget look.

Racks

Racks are wire or wood display cases that stand alone or hang from retail wall paneling called slat walls. Slat walls have also been used throughout the salon industry since we can remember. Many salon owners are replacing their rack display cases with stand-alone gondolas or display cases that match the materials used in the rest of the salon. Doing so gives cohesiveness throughout the salon, giving the retail department a better fit and feel for your customers and staff.

Round Rack

These are circular in design and can vary in size and diameter. Most can be adjusted for the height of the product displayed. Round racks hold a great amount of product and should be used for promotional items.

Cubes

This type of shelving is a freestanding product display. They come in many different sizes. They are a wonderful way to promote one specific product. You must have a good amount of space to use these effectively.

Tables

For flexibility, a few tables that provide a flat surface for seasonal displays or special offers may be a good idea. Portables are commonly used when you are having a sale or for samples. The nice thing about this is when you have a promotion you can easily take them away when you are done. They can also travel with you

NOTE

Tables are also known as impulse tables. Great for moving sale items!!

to exhibits and shows that you might attend for bridal shows, Chamber of Commerce events, or beauty school presentations/recruiting days.

Bins, Barrels, & Baskets

Another set of fixtures that offer flexibility are bins, barrels, and baskets. They can easily be moved or relocated throughout the salon and allow you to keep your retail area looking fresh and new.

Bins, barrels, and baskets are a great way to display samples and/or items that you may want to discontinue. Use these sparingly because cluttering up your retail area is not an effective look in a salon and can have a negative effect on sales.

Salon Owner/Operators Discuss the Good, the Bad, & the Ugly

Salon Owner C.G. Horton

"Make sure there isn't any emptiness!! Fill it slap full with one or two product lines."

Sue Gahr, Point Pleasant, NJ

"My retail area looks beautiful. I change my display for holidays and seasons. My customers stop, look, and buy. I always get compliments on how my retail area looks. Selling retail has become my passion."

CHAPTER 13

Used Salon Furniture & Equipment—Getting Creative

Believe it or not, there is a big market for used salon furniture and equipment. It might just take some research to find the right place or the right person who is remodeling their salon. You never know; their "trash" might be your treasure. People who are remodeling want to get rid of what they have. The equipment dealer in the area probably offered them "next to nothing" for it; so, they decided to sell it on their own. This is a good opportunity to save some money. Here are different ways to locate used furniture.

- Craigslist (www.craigslist.com): Find your local or regional area on the site.
- Local newspapers: go to the classified section and look under furniture.
- eBay: check out the site, you might find some used furniture available.
- Salon furniture supplier: you never know when they might have clearance or slightly used items for sale.

It is important to realize that there are limitations to used equipment. We don't recommend buying any used plumbing products, unless you have the history on the item. We also don't recommend buying any electrical products, such as a multifunction skincare machine. All of these items will not have a warranty when bought used and parts may be nonexistent.

> **NOTE**
>
> We recommend that you only buy used equipment from a local source so you can test and look closely at the merchandise before you buy it.

Consider used furniture for guest seating, styling chairs, skincare tables, or workstations. However, if you are mixing and matching old and new, then putting the used items throughout your salon can save you a lot of money.

On the following page is a chart comparing the differences in used and new costs for budget-priced versus expensive furniture and equipment. As mentioned in a previous chapter, you might be able to get better pricing from someone who is remodeling and is desperate to sell their old furniture and equipment. The prices below are slightly higher because, in this case, the seller is putting the product on the market, but is not desperately seeking a buyer. Keep in mind that the prices below do not include any type of shipping or delivery.

Furniture Comparison				
	Budget		Expensive	
	Used	New	Used	New
Styling chairs	$75.00	$175.00	$200.00	$600.00
Dryer chairs	$150.00	$350.00	$200.00	$700.00
Sink	$75.00	$175.00	$175.00	$400.00
Shampoo chair	$50.00	$125.00	$125.00	$350.00
Reception desk	$150.00	$400.00	$400.00	$2,000.00
Retail unit	$100.00	$250.00	$300.00	$900.00
Reception chairs	$25.00	$80.00	$100.00	$350.00
Nail table	$50.00	$140.00	$125.00	$600.00
Styling stations	$50.00	$150.00	$200.00	$600.00
Clothes washer	$100.00	$400.00	NA	NA
Clothes dryer	$100.00	$400.00	NA	NA
Pedicure unit	$200.00	$600.00	$500.00	$2,500.00
Stools	$25.00	$75.00	$50.00	$200.00
Facial steamer	$75.00	$180.00	$150.00	$450.00
Magnifying lamp	$50.00	$150.00	$100.00	$300.00
Facial table	$75.00	$200.00	$300.00	$1,000.00
Multi-function unit	$200.00	$600.00	$300.00	$2,000.00
Sink vanity	$50.00	$200.00	$150.00	$500.00
Shampoo cabinet	$100.00	$300.00	$200.00	$600.00
Shampoo unit and chair	$150.00	$500.00	$400.00	$2,000.00
Make up unit	$50.00	$200.00	$250.00	$1,000.00
Color trolley	$25.00	$80.00	$75.00	$250.00
TOTALS	$1,925.00	$5,730.00	$4,300.00	$17,300.00

Salon Owner/Operators Discuss the Good, the Bad, & the Ugly

Sue Holmann, All About You Hair and Nail Spa

"I found used massage tables and facial equipment on Craigslist. It was almost brand new at a third of the price. It allowed me to experiment with spa services at a fraction of the cost. I had two empty rooms; now, they produce revenue that I did not expect."

CHAPTER 14

Selecting the Right Architect & Contractor

Congratulations! You have come a long way. The lease process and negotiations are finished. You have worked with a salon designer to lay out your salon. Next on the list is selecting the right architect and contractor. If you are in a shopping center, your landlord may be able to direct you to an architect and contractor they have used before.

Finding & Working With an Architect

First, you will need an architect to get you started. This individual will help design and space-plan your location. You can find businesses that specialize in space-planning and design that also sell salon furniture. We highly recommend that you find one of these companies and space-plan your salon before you go to the architect. You will save money with the architect if you get your space-plan done elsewhere. The architect, who is not likely to have experience in designing salons, won't have to spend time researching how to space-plan a salon.

Here are a couple of websites to help you locate an architect:

- **www.architectfinder.aia.org**
- **www.servicemagic.com**

The architect will draw up the blueprints for your new space. It is critical for you to spend a lot of time with the architect to make sure he or she puts everything in the right place.

Once you have the architect's plans, you should move quickly to get some prices on the cost for construction. You want to bid your job and get prices from at least three contractors. You should plan on giving each contractor four to five sets of plans so they can rapidly get you a final price. Ask your architect to make 15 sets of plans. It sounds like a lot, but this will save you weeks of time. A contractor usually takes a set of plans, leaves them with a plumber, electrician, and an air conditioning company, and calls them back in a few days for their price. If you only get five sets of plans, you can only give one to two sets to each contractor, which will make the bidding/pricing process take longer.

Next, you will choose your contractor. We all understand that price is a BIG factor, but we must look at each contractor's bid and compare. We must make sure that each bid includes everything on the plan. We must reiterate that a contractor is only as good as the plans he works from. If the plan is not complete or is missing something, a contractor will do the work, but also charge you for the change. It can be very costly. Before you take the finished plan from the architect, it's important to review it and make sure every detail is included.

Your architect will also give you two copies of "certified plans." These plans are the ones that your chosen contractor will submit to the city. Do not misplace or mix them up with any other copies.

Finding & Working With the Contractor

You have spent hours with the architect going over plans and discussing so many different ideas and layouts. You are confident that your ideas are finally down on paper and that you have the look you want. Just one question remains, "Who is going to build it?"

Friends, family, and associates can usually recommend a good contractor. If you cannot find someone you feel comfortable with, you can try these websites:

- **www.1800contractor.com**
- **www.needacontractor.com**
- **www.agc.org**

To help with your contractor selection, we have put together the most important questions you should ask your potential contractor before you hire them.

When selecting and working with contractors, be sure to:

○ **Ask what type of projects they have done.** Many contractors have done various projects, but have they ever built out a salon? Do they specialize in cabinetry, or are they more of a generalist that does a bit of everything? If they concentrate on remodeling projects and deal with a variety of subcontractors, plumbers, and electricians, they may be a good fit for your project. A contractor that builds custom homes may not be the wise choice for a salon build-out or remodel on a tight budget.

○ **Visit some existing or recently completed projects.** Good builders are proud of their projects. Ask to see photographs or visit the contractor's last project. Talk with the client; ask how the contractor handled the job and whether they are happy with the outcome of the project.

○ **Get a list of former clients.** Word of mouth is often the best solution when hiring a contractor or builder. If the contractor gives you five people to call, make sure you call all of them and ask what type of relationship they had with the contractor and would they work with the contractor again.

○ **Check that he is licensed and insured!** In today's world, you should never hire a contractor who is not licensed and insured. This should protect you against any accidents and/or liabilities that may arise during your remodel or build-out. More importantly, if a contractor bears the expense of carrying the cost of the license and insurance, they are most likely a professional company. Also, if you're borrowing money from a bank, they will require that your contractor has the necessary insurance and license. They will not give you the money needed for your construction if your contractor doesn't carry general liability and Workers' Compensation Insurance.

○ **Ask how long he has been in business.** The fact that a builder or contractor has been in business more than five years is a good thing. It is an indication that the builder can run a successful project and satisfy customers.

○ **Find out who will be running your project.** This is very important. If you build a relationship with your contractor, you will feel better if he is on the job every day. If he uses subcontractors and he is going to manage from an office or the back of his truck, you can bet you will not be happy. Smaller contractors are more likely to provide a hands-on approach, which is probably the best option for keeping your project on time and on budget.

○ **Confirm payment terms.** Contractors get paid in many different ways. Before the project starts, agree to terms and sign a written contract on how you are expected to pay.

○ **Never pay in advance or in full.** You always want to stay ahead of your contractor. If you owe your contractor, it ensures that they will complete whatever task is on hand. You will have deadlines to meet. Be sure they will be there for inspections or anything else that comes up. I have heard many horror stories about disappearing contractors.

It is important to choose your contractor in a timely fashion for a few reasons:

1. At this stage, you will probably have already signed the lease and the clock is ticking on the "free" rent period that you may have negotiated for the build-out. One way to get around this is to negotiate with the landlord and not to pay rent until you get your final "Certificate of Occupancy" (CO) from the city. You can also negotiate with the landlord to start your free rent after your CO (refer to Chapter 5).

2. Your contractor will be the one to submit the plans to the city. In our past experience, this can take anywhere from two to six weeks. The city can also reject the plans, which will have to go back to the architect and be resubmitted.

3. The process might take a couple of weeks to get final bids from your three prospective contractors.

<table><tr><td>Salon Owner/Operators Discuss the Good, the Bad, & the Ugly</td><td>

James Giodano, Fancy and Prancy Hair

"Choosing a family member as your contractor may save you a few dollars. But what happens when the work is not getting done on time or the quality of the work is not what you expected? I had to fire my wife's brother. It's been two years and he still doesn't talk to me."</td></tr></table>

The Construction Phase

Construction can be the most costly when building your salon. If you have had any kind of construction done, you know that overruns and lack of knowledge on your part can be expensive. To help keep you from unforeseen expenses and issues during the construction phase, we have identified some of the most common things that you'll need to modify in a typical location.

You should also realize that all of these upgrades can be negotiated with the landlord and become his expense, not yours. We recommend that you look at the space very closely and ask the landlord or the leasing agent what the store has and what the lease includes.

Air Conditioning

A typical location in a shopping center usually has an air conditioning unit that is inadequate for a salon. Below are what the landlord typically gives and what the salon needs:

- Typical space: one ton for every 400 square feet
- Recommended size: one ton for every 180 square feet

If the landlord does not want to increase the capacity of your A/C unit, then there will be a cost of $1500 to $2000 per ton of A/C to increase the size. Each location should be checked thoroughly.

Electrical

The standard-size panel in a normal store is usually 125 amps. That amount is too small and a decent size salon needs a panel of 250 amps. Upgrading electrical can get very expensive.

To increase an electrical panel, you need to run more wires from the main electrical room in the shopping center. If it's 400 feet away from your space, it will be thousands of dollars to bring in more power. Check your location very carefully.

If you are thinking of renting an older building, wiring may need to be replaced and upgraded to meet the present building codes. This alone can easily run thousands of dollars.

Plumbing

Have the right number of bathrooms to meet state requirements is the biggest issue. If you have six stylists or more, most states/counties require two bathrooms. It usually costs about $5000 to put in a bathroom.

You are best off following the requirements of the state or county. Besides, the second bathroom can double as a changing room. If you look at an 8-station salon, you can have as many as 25 people in it at any given time. One bathroom is inadequate.

Many times, existing bathrooms do not meet the latest handicap accessibility codes. The county may ask you to make it bigger, change the toilet, and/or put in a sink that works for wheelchairs. You may have to install handicap rails if they are not there already. Your county may also ask you to install a ramp for access to the bathrooms if your salon has any kind of elevation. The latest codes are for the door to be 36 inches wide and to open out with a lever handle only. The inside must have a 44 inch clearance for a wheelchair to completely turn around in the bathroom. The pipes underneath the sink must have heat-resistant covers to protect a handicapped person's legs when they are underneath the sink.

Another common plumbing issue is the size of the hot water heater. Usually it is too small for a salon. A salon needs a minimum of an 80 gallon, double-element water heater. Anything less will create a hot water shortage in your salon. The cost is around $500 for an electric water heater. If you have the potential of using a natural gas water heater, this will be more efficient.

Also, remember that you will need a washer (and a dryer) for towels. You will want to make sure that your space can accommodate this addition.

Shampoo Area

It is recommended that this be located near the bathroom or dispensary for two reasons. One, if there is an existing floor, this usually needs to be cut up to install your waste water pipes underneath. The water always needs a downward flow toward the drain; water cannot flow upwards to drain. This may not be an issue if you have a basement.

Second, your hot water heater is usually located in the dispensary. If your sinks are far away from that, you have the potential of losing "hot water" and you will be washing your clients with "cold water." It may be solved by insulating the water lines. Either way, it will cost you more money.

Drywall or Partition Construction

When searching for a facility, it is preferred that all the walls are open to add electrical, telephone, Internet, and alarms inside the walls before you close them up. Of course, this all depends on the location and whether the location is new or existing. When considering your existing bathroom, this may not be up to code on the size, which means you will have to tear down the existing walls and rebuild the bathroom.

If you're in an older building and your walls are made out of plaster and lathe, it can be very expensive to move walls and make any alterations.

Lighting

The most cost-effective type of ceiling lighting is the standard 2x2 or 2x4 acoustical ceiling lights. They may not be the most attractive, but it will save you thousands of dollars in a year. We have seen clients use many types of halogen lights. Halogen lights work very well, but this will really increase your budget. The standard ceiling is usually included when you take the store. If it's not new construction, you may need to replace the covers for the typical fluorescent lights. They may be yellow and look unsightly. You may not have enough lighting in the styling area and have to add more lights, not something many people realize. These can be negotiated with the landlord if you realize the shortage or the yellowing before you sign your lease.

Reference: www.salonlights.com & www.freestylist.com

> **NOTE**
>
> Lighting is evolving and new systems are being introduced to the salon marketplace. So, keep watch for what is new and what might save you money in the long run.

Ceiling

A landlord will usually give you a standard 2x4 acoustical ceiling. Many clients have chosen to go with no ceiling. Beware, leaving an open ceiling will greatly increase your electric bill for A/C or heat over the year. Plus, with all of the duct work and lighting, dust begins to build and every 6 months you will need a crew to come in and clean it. If you don't schedule regular cleanings, the salon will begin to look dirty and unsightly. Most salons paint their ceilings black, to give an open "infinity" feeling, but this shows dirt immediately.

Flooring

Wood, ceramic tile, and rubber are suitable floor types. Our experience has been that all the floors can look amazing in your salon; it all depends on the budget you want to spend. One thing you should consider, especially in the shampoo area: water will spill on the floor and once it gets wet, it might become slippery and create a liability issue. When choosing your flooring, remember that whatever product you choose, it must be durable, not slippery when wet, and good on the feet and legs for an extended period of time.

> **NOTE**
>
> Stained concrete is the latest trend. It is very durable, but it is hard on the feet and back.

CHAPTER 16

Computerizing Your Salon

Written by John Harms, President/Founder Meevo (Millennium).

Computerizing your salon can be very intimidating. This chapter will help you answer questions like:

- Why computerize at all?
- When should I start worrying about my software and computers?
- What is a typical plan for computerizing a salon?
- Which software should I buy?
- What about ongoing training and support?
- Which computers do I need? Do I need a server? If so, how many other computers should I have?
- What kind of additional hardware would I want to consider (i.e., cash drawers)?

Why Computerize at All?

Computers have been used in some salons since 1980; however, the penetration into the beauty industry didn't really take hold until the turn of the century. Most people simply used cash registers or a computer as a cash register. As software became more powerful and appointment books could be written that looked and functioned like a true appointment book, the industry began to embrace technology more.

Let's face it. The appointment book is the lifeblood of many salons. The scariest thing for any salon owner or manager is the act of replacing their paper-based appointment book and putting the pencils and eraser shavings under the desk. However, within a week or two of being computerized, salon owners who made the switch tell us they would never turn back. Here are just a few reasons:

- No more asking the client repeatedly for their name and phone number even though they've come to you for years.
- Automated pre-booking of the client's next appointment.
- Quick ways to move an appointment between employees or days.
- Automated wait lists.
- Instant statistics on percent booked, pre-booked, and more.
- Visualization (by color) of what type of appointment it is.
- Automated confirmations of appointments.
- Create standing appointments in seconds—not hours!

The top three reasons to automate your salon are:

1. Professionalism and ability to serve your clients efficiently.

2. Enhanced ability to grow and market your business.

3. Security and control.

Yes, integrating credit card processing and other great features are helpful, but you should look at automation as an opportunity to grow your salon business. Client loyalty systems, automated email marketing, online booking, gift card purchasing, and other great features help make your business special. Differentiating yourself with memberships, VIP rewards, special pricing, and direct access to your clients via things like text messaging specials or appointment openings can help you retain more clients.

The bottom line—a salon that is not computerized cannot serve their clients at the same level as a fully computerized salon.

Everything is smoother and faster:

- Calls to book or change an appointment
- Ring-up with integrated credit card processing
- Looking up gift card balances

Think about how much time it would take to look up the hair color formula for a client using the old-style card files. Using the computer, it would take a matter of seconds. In fact, the computer would know WHICH formula to print out with the daily appointment for a smoother process and seamless service experience for the client.

When Should You Start Worrying About Software & Computers?

Many people think they need to wait until the salon is almost ready to open before ordering computers and software. You actually want to plan your computerization as early as the initial architectural phase of your build-out. So many times, salon owners underestimate the space required on a desk for monitors, receipt printers, credit card swipe machines, keyboards, and mice. Also, you need to plan the appropriate placement of simple things like grommet holes to hide wires on top of the desk. All-in-one computers and wireless hardware can reduce some of the clutter, but knowing which computers will be used is important when purchasing or building the front desk.

Getting a jump start on data entry is a good idea. You'll be able to use any customer data for pre-opening marketing. You need to enter all of your products and barcodes into the system, prices, employees, existing client records, employee schedules, and commission structures. The list goes on and on. It's not an overwhelming task, but it's certainly not something you want to wait to do until the week before you open! Also, you will want to have your staff trained on the new system prior to opening. Many times, the data entry is done off-site at another location while the construction phase is underway. Then, once the "dirty" part of the construction is done, the computers, network, and other hardware are brought in to be installed.

Which Software Should You Choose?

Choosing the right software package comes down to asking the right questions of the software company and yourself. Are you looking for a simple cash register system that gives you some basic reports? If yes, you need to rethink what a computer can do for you. It needs to be more than an appointment book and more than a point-of-sale system. The great news is most software is quite affordable compared to 10 years ago. Many software systems offer subscriptions with little or no money down for a monthly fee that includes support and updates. Be sure to check out the options and pricing models available to you.

Keep in mind, however, that over 50 percent of people who purchase software don't pick the right one the first time. They either overlook key features that are missing or find that the software they purchased isn't ready to grow with them. Then, it's back to the drawing board to research and buy another software package and transfer the data or reenter it! Sound painful? It can be! So, take the time to evaluate your needs, research the software, and— more importantly—research the company behind the software prior to purchasing.

To build a successful salon, you'll need to keep tabs on five key metrics or key performance indicators:

1. New Clients Per Month
2. New Client Retention
3. Repeat Client Retention

4. Frequency of Visit

5. Average Ticket

Your software must have these metrics to give you the forward focus view of how your business is doing. All software tracks how much revenue you are making in services, retail, gift cards, packages, and so forth. Revenue is important, but it's based on what you did yesterday to grow your business.

The "growth indicators" are the metrics of what you can expect in revenue tomorrow. The beauty is you can affect them today, in the moment, and throughout the day by pre-booking clients and doing the right thing to retain the clients you worked so hard to bring in. Follow the growth indicators on a weekly basis and you'll see your business grow organically one client at a time.

What Is a Typical Plan for Computerizing a Salon?

Unfortunately, there is not a one-size-fits-all solution when it comes to setting up your salon to be fully automated. Many factors, like size, number of network connections, and number of workstations (connected computers), affect the planning. However, you will take some definite steps and need to meet key milestones to get your technology infrastructure in place.

Phase I: Research

- Utilize the Internet to search for salon software or salon management software. You'll find dozens of options available to you. Look for companies that have been around for more than a couple of years and have shown a dedication to the beauty industry. Many companies come and go and you don't want to invest in a fly-by-night company.

- Ask around at industry events. What are other people using? Do they like it? Do they feel they get input into the updates? Does the company have annual conferences and attend industry-specific educational events?

Phase II: Demo/Testing

- Download a trial version of the software or request a demo.

- Schedule a live demonstration with a salesperson and gauge their knowledge of the beauty industry.

- Ask for the support phone number and try it a few times before you buy. Does someone answer? Do they know what they are talking about? Do they know the industry? Are they friendly and helpful?

Phase III: Software Selection

• After determining the top three software companies that fit your needs, you'll have to evaluate them on price, length of time in business, number of support staff, features/ benefits of the software, and overall feeling you get for the company.

• Once you make a selection, it still takes a few phone calls and decisions before you're ready to start installing the software and entering data.

Phase IV: Hardware Needs Assessment

• It's best if you choose a company that is also knowledgeable in hardware, computers, and the other devices you'll need to run a successful salon.

• Ask for a needs assessment based on the size of your salon, size of your front desk, number of employees, and budget.

Phase V: Hardware Purchase

• Some computers, when special ordered, take a couple of weeks to ship. When they arrive, the software company can usually install the software for you. So, expect up to four weeks for computer delivery. It can come faster if the computers are in stock, but that's not always the case, especially during the busy season.

• During this phase, you should contact local computer service technicians to begin forging a relationship for ongoing support, computer setup, etc.

Phase VI: Network Setup

• You need to decide if you want to run wires for a wired network, which results in faster access to your data. However, if you want to run a wireless system, you will have to purchase computers and an operating system that will work best with a wireless system.

Phase VII: Software Installation

• Your software may be preinstalled on the computers you purchased from your provider. However, if you purchased the computers on your own, you'll need to install the software.

• Even if the software you are using is Web-based, there is still configuration and installation of drivers for your equipment.

Phase VIII: Data Entry Training

• Before you start entering data, take the time to get proper training or read the manual on how to enter the data properly.

Phase IX: Data Entry or Data Conversion

- Start pulling old invoices, purchase orders, and service menus together so you can enter them into the software you've purchased.

- Divide the work up amongst your staff so that everyone learns. However, make sure they enter the data consistently. It's important to make sure the data goes in properly so that the reports you run make sense.

- If you are doing a data conversion, see the section later in this chapter on handling your data conversion.

Phase X: Advanced Training & Practice

- Now that your data is entered, you want to get advanced training on the appointment book, register, inventory, management, and security.

- Practice! Some software comes with the ability to create an instance of your data so you can train your employees and practice using the system without affecting the actual data.

Phase XI: Testing for "Go Live"

- Prior to going "live" and opening your salon for business with the new system, go through some sample ring-ups, bookings, payrolls, etc. to verify the system is functioning and set up properly.

Phase XII: "Go Live!"

- Fire up the computers and start booking appointments and ringing up all of those sales! Remember, partner with a software company that focuses on making the front desk a power position that helps grow the business!

Data Conversion & Set Up

Once your software is installed, it is time to prepare for your training on the software. If you are going to convert data from an existing software application, **it is HIGHLY recommended that a preliminary conversion is performed.** A preliminary conversion will allow you to perform your training on the software using your real data. The conversion will give you the opportunity to identify any issues with your conversion and what "tasks" you will need to accomplish once your final conversion has been performed.

Ask your software provider if they have a task sheet specific to your conversion on typical items that should be handled either before or after your conversion. It will save you a lot of time and money if your software provider identifies the key issues that need to be addressed.

Also, ask your software provider if they have an implementation department. That department is specifically designed to walk you through the process of implementing your software and getting you live. They will make sure everything is set for you from the installation of the software, to scheduling your conversions, to performing follow-up calls on the day you go live, which will help ensure this process is as painless as possible.

One key thing to note is that not all software companies have full conversions from other software companies. It is possible that you can lose your client history and that you'll need to start from scratch or enter all the data manually.

It's very important to ask what major data WILL be converted and what major data WILL NOT be converted. For example, in some circumstances, the software company may only be able to convert client information and this would result in a one-time only conversion.

Another important fact for you to consider is that the software company may not be able to convert any data directly from your current software. However, you should find out if there are exporting capabilities via reports or any other method. Your new software company may be able to create custom conversions for you if the data exported is in a readable format.

Once the software is installed or your preliminary conversion has been implemented, you are ready to begin your training and determine a "go-live" date. Use this date and work backward to come up with a training schedule. Be sure to check if there are any scheduled staff vacations, holidays, or anything else that may hinder your plan. If your software company has an implementation department, they will be more than happy to work on a game plan for you. As long as you and your staff accomplish your "homework" during your training sessions, you will be able to go live as planned.

Training & Support

How your data is entered and set up from the start will shape how your reports are viewed, how your front desk operates, and how your appointment book will be viewed by all. Most software companies only include a basic training package with the purchase of the software. Be sure to ask what training package options are available to you in order to make an informed decision as to what will be best for your business needs.

If your business is brand-new, the basic training package is usually enough for you to get started. There will be many distractions when opening a new business. Just focusing on the basics of the software is more important than trying to learn everything or using every feature. You should schedule more advanced training later on—once your salon has been up and running for a few months.

However, if you are operating an established business with refined processes, the basic training package will not be enough for you. You will require additional training time to fully understand how your new software handles your current procedures. In some cases, the new software will not be able to generate the same reports as before or may not have a feature you were accustomed to using. It's very important you receive additional training time to review current procedures and policies, as this will allow you to update your current training guides for each department.

Your training sessions should be broken up into two groups: management and employee. To keep labor costs down, only include people in training when there is reason to have them present. For example, there is no need to include service providers or front desk staff if you are learning how to enter employee commissions into the software. Be sure to ask what will be covered during each training session so you can include only the appropriate personnel.

DO NOT leave one person in charge of learning the software and setting everything up for your business—that approach always fails. If you place a newly-hired manager, friend, or existing long-time employee in charge of setting up the most important aspect of your business, they will become too stressed. They'll leave, start to hate the new software, hate their job, or contaminate other employees to hate the new software. You'll end up having a coup on your hands and a mess to clean up.

That might be an over-exaggeration of what could happen; but the point is, use caution if you are thinking this is one person's responsibility. Include yourself, as the business owner, in these training sessions to keep the momentum going and the frustration level controlled. It will also allow you to make sure the employee or employees in charge of handling this new software installation have the necessary time needed to make this a successful installation.

It is highly recommended that you receive an estimate for the cost of having a software trainer come to your facility and assist with the training/launch of the software. If you have the budget, this approach is 99 percent effective when it comes to making sure your training is a success. All processes are considered and implemented. Your operations and your clientele may only be minimally affected by this conversion. Having a trainer onsite, who knows the software, can help you during the go live process and ensure that your cash drawers balance to the penny from the very first day.

With any technology change or installation, you can expect bumps in the road. But, having a knowledgeable resource at your facility will be priceless and ensure the success of your software implementation.

Ongoing Training

Once the dust has settled and you've started to master the basics of your software application, it's time to revisit the multitude of other features that the software offers. These may be advanced features that caught your attention at the time of purchase. They may include automation of client loyalty programs and allowing clients to earn points for purchases or book appointments online.

Ask your software provider what additional training options are offered. In most cases, such packages are available via DVDs, online Webinars, or additional remote training sessions that have been customized to your desired topics of discussion. Even better, most software companies offer an Annual User Group Conference where you can attend a forum for only current users of the same software. They get together and discuss what they have done with the software to make their business a success and what improvements they would like to see in future versions.

If your software company has an online community forum, we highly recommend you be active on the site and read what others are discussing. The ability to discuss with other business owners in your industry how to implement something new or discuss compensation strategies and hear what has worked and what hasn't will be invaluable to you.

Always be aware of what your software company's rollout plan is for releasing software updates and learn how you can find out what has been addressed/enhanced in the update. Most users think that updates are made to apply fixes to issues. But, many times, new features or reporting capabilities are also released at the same time. The new features are usually released to meet current trends and user requirements. A software release often means new metrics or capabilities to improve your front desk operations and improve your bottom line.

Hardware

Let's look at some of the hardware you might need to purchase and some of the questions you might have about technology.

Computers

- Do I need a "real" server? No. If you are just looking to have a small network without online booking or an online store, you can use a fileserver or robust workstation to act as your server. Larger network servers are recommended for:
  - Five or more computers
  - Several open connections for online booking
  - Multiple and different types of software running at the same time

- How many workstations should I get? The answer depends upon the amount of staff and space you have. In an average-sized salon, there would be two computers at the front desk for reservations and check out and another computer in the back for a look-up station and to import service notes for the staff.

- Do I need a computer in the backroom? It is highly recommended to eliminate clutter and personnel swarming at the front desk by having a "look-up station" in the back of the salon. Your front desk is a client's first impression. It's best to eliminate as much chaos at the front desk as possible. When employees have a source of checking on appointments and monitoring their metrics, it promotes a more relaxed atmosphere and more informed service providers.

Network

- Wired or wireless? Wired networks are ideal in most scenarios. The data transfer rate is higher and it requires less maintenance than a wireless network. However, wireless networks can be used with tools like Microsoft® Terminal Services and ThinSoft® WinConnect®, allowing you to use portable tablet PCs or eliminate the clutter of wired stations.

- Should I get an Internet connection? The Internet is essential to taking advantage of email and social media marketing, remote backups, and for doing automated updates. It is also an essential element to allow remote support by your software company.

Peripheral Equipment

- Cash Drawers: You can choose between USB and serial cash drawers. It is suggested that you purchase USB drawers, as most computers don't come with serial ports anymore. Cash drawers add a layer of security to your front desk because they are locked unless the computer opens the drawer. Each time that occurs, the software you choose should track it in an activity log for your review.

- Receipt Printers: Most receipt printers work well with salon software. You may want to purchase a receipt printer that has a mechanism to automatically open your cash drawer, which will allow you to purchase a non-intelligent drawer and save money.

- Other equipment: You might consider a credit card swipe that mounts on the side of your monitor; pole displays to show what the client is purchasing (this is a requirement in certain states or counties); paging systems that alert staff when a client checks in; and more. You might be surprised at all the options you have once you computerize.

Third-Party Vendors

Software companies typically align themselves with third-party partners to enhance the company's offerings as well as negotiate rates and costs on the client's behalf. These third-party vendors either integrate directly with the software or offer products and services that conform to the standards of growth and development that the software was designed to offer.

It's very important to learn about the people and companies who are affiliated with the software company and come with such great references. Integrity is everything in this business and only the best software company will align themselves with the best third-party partners. Some examples of third-party involvement or integrations can include, but are not limited to, credit card processing, gift cards and online certificates, and even advanced marketing support.

Credit Card Processing

Software and Point-of-Sale (POS) applications should have the capability to process credit and debit cards directly through the system. Although the functionality exists, the salon would still need to establish a merchant account with the recommended third-party partner.

What is a merchant account? It is a specific account set up with a financial institution to allow you to accept credit card payments directly from your clients. You need a merchant account if you want to take credit card payments from your clients through your business name and have the money deposited directly into your business checking account.

There are a variety of merchant acquirers. So, ask the right questions to help ensure that you are receiving the best possible rates, care, and customer service.

✓ CHECK IT OUT

Check off the questions below as you ask them.

○ Is there an application fee?

○ Is there a programming or setup fee?

○ What are the "other" fees associated with my merchant account?

○ Are the quoted rates guaranteed? If so, for how long?

○ Is there a contract? If so, for how long?

○ Are there any termination fees or early cancellation fees?

○ If there is a problem, who do I talk to?

○ How long do processed payments take to reach my bank account?

○ Are there any reserve requirements or hold backs? Can I get that in writing?

○ What are the hours of operation for customer service?

Gift Cards & Online Gift Certificates

Software and Point-of-Sale (POS) applications should have the capability to integrate with a magnetic strip or bar-coded gift card solution. Gift cards represent your company's brand. The recommended third-party partner should offer a turnkey solution from graphic design to production.

You need a partner with the flexibility and the power to execute a distinct, exciting gift card program that engages and excites your guests, enhances your brand, and strengthens your bottom line. Gift cards are a necessity and considered a "must have" when opening a new salon. They are a perfect solution for day-to-day traffic (peer-to-peer interaction). However, a solution must also be considered for Internet and online traffic (non-peer-to-peer traffic).

The solution is quite easy: offer your clients the ability to purchase gift certificates online. This capability is a great service for your clients, providing convenience, instant gratification, and solving last-minute, gift-giving problems. You'll sell more gift certificates and save staff time while doing it. A variety of companies provide this service. Asking the right questions will help ensure that you are receiving the best possible rates, care, and customer service.

Check off the questions below as you ask them.

- ○ Why do I need your gift card services?
- ○ What will the gift certificates look like?
- ○ How does it work?
- ○ How does it affect my front desk staff?
- ○ Who typically buys Instant gift certificates?
- ○ How are credit cards processed online?
- ○ How will my clients receive their gift certificates purchased online?
- ○ Can I run specials or promotions?
- ○ How are gratuities handled?
- ○ What percentage or profit-share do you charge on purchases?

Marketing Support

Software and Point-of-Sale (POS) applications should provide a variety of key marketing and tracking techniques that should help you improve the frequency of visits from your clientele, target new clients, identify clients who are due in for services, and a lot more! These specific features should lead to increased revenue and client satisfaction.

However, the reality is that the software or POS application is a "supporting cast" under the overall marketing umbrella. Other marketing and branding methods not handled by the software or POS application, include, but are not limited to: social media, search engine optimization, and website development. You will need more advanced/strategic campaigns for promoting your brand, offerings, and specials that extend beyond the capabilities and features of the software or POS application.

As a new business owner, you may find yourself inundated with everything from staffing, to furniture, to software, and POS application research. You're only one person and you can't do everything yourself. In addition, your budget may not allow you to hire an in-house marketing specialist/director to help take care of these essential marketing tasks.

This is a perfect opportunity to seek out referrals or recommended business partners from your software or POS application. Leverage their expertise and years of experience within the industry to find out what works and what doesn't. The level of commitment to the industry by the software or POS application vendor should be further emphasized by the affiliates they recommend for marketing and advertising support.

CHAPTER 17

Credit Card Processing—Selecting the Right Partner

Written by Guy Wadas, National Sales Director, Integrity Payment Systems.

Understanding credit card processing and knowing how to leverage its advantages can have a dramatic, profitable impact for salon owners. Choosing the wrong credit card processor or not understanding the best way to structure your processor agreement can be a constant monthly drain on your business.

Most businesses—no matter how large or small—make very small profits on a percentage basis. Knowing how to increase your profits—even by a percentage point or two—can provide the difference between "getting by" and enjoying a business which provides you with the lifestyle you want.

Following is an overview of the reasons to accept credit cards, the costs and benefits of credit card processing, how to select the right processor, and what questions to ask before signing any agreement. At the end of the chapter, we will also provide a list of unique programs offered to salon owners by one credit card processing company, including a free assessment of your current costs.

Why Accept Credit Cards?

For some salon owners, operating on a strictly cash basis seems like the least costly way to operate. No processing fees, no equipment to buy—and, it seems clean and simple. In fact, in the early 1990s, more than 80 percent of the money coming into salons was in the form of cash. Now, however, that number has flipped and more than 80 percent of the money coming into salons is through credit or check/debit cards. Why the switch? It's all about convenience for the customer and the potential additional profits for the salon owner.

Everything has a cost. Identifying the cost of credit card processing on the balance sheet is easy to do. What is not easy is to identify the cost of NOT accepting credit cards in your business. Several studies have shown that customers are willing to spend more when paying with credit than when paying with cash. In fact, when J. C. Penney Company, Inc. started to accept credit cards in its stores several years ago, it found that the average transaction for credit customers was $50 compared to cash transactions of only $20. People are not carrying cash these days; instead, they want the convenience of paying with credit or debit cards.

Salon owners can capitalize on this by offering customers products as well as add-on services. When paying with credit, customers are much more likely to purchase a service package, gift certificates/cards, as well as retail and boutique items. Walk-in customers are also likely to prefer to pay with credit by the same 80/20 ratio. Referring these customers to a nearby ATM machine sends the message that you are more concerned about your convenience than your customers. Many will not come back to an establishment that does not accept payment via credit/debit card. The cost of NOT accepting credit may be the loss of sales in additional products and services over months and years, and you could lose the 80 percent of customers who no longer prefer to pay with cash.

If it makes sense to accept credit and debit card payments in your salon, how do you make sure you do this in a way that is best for you, rather than your bank or a third-party processor?

Choosing the Right Processor

Your local bank may provide credit processing either directly or through a third-party processor. You can also contract directly with a processor like Integrity Payment Systems. Who you choose for this important process can make a huge difference in your bottom-line profits.

Most local banks outsource this service to a third party that has an agreement or arrangement with the bank. A few national banks process credit transactions themselves. Regardless, you need to ask several key questions in order to make sure you have the best program for your business.

If the processing is outsourced, it is likely the customer service will also be outsourced. That can create a very frustrating situation should you have a problem or question. Look for a full-service credit card processor that handles not only the sales, but also the back-end processing, customer service, and other functions. They will be the most secure when it comes to protecting your customers' sensitive credit card information. They will also be the most responsive should you ever have an issue.

Is the Lowest Rate Always Best?

Most processors will quote a rate for processing transactions and position a rate that is one of the lowest rates available. What they do not tell you is the additional fees that are involved, including a substantial cancellation or early-termination fee designed to keep you locked into the contract even after you find a better provider. Low rates can be deceiving. Be sure you understand all the terms in the contract.

You want to get to a number called "total cost" or "effective rate." That number includes not only the low rate, but all of the add-on charges, fees, and other costs. The effective rate is the number that matters, not the initial rate.

Card companies such as Visa, MasterCard, Discover, and American Express set different rates for different cards, industries, and customers. These rates are called interchange. They are numerous, and to further complicate the picture, these rates range anywhere from a zero percentage rate with a small per-item fee, to levels that include a percentage rate greater than three percent with large per-item fees. Unless you are working with a company that specializes in the salon industry, it is unlikely you will be able to obtain the most favorable rates for a salon business. In fact, you will most likely be quoted the same rates and pricing structures as the car repair shop down the street. One size does not fit all, and one rate for all businesses is not going to fit either.

Integrity Payment Systems has been monitoring the flow of transactions for the salon industry for many years. Your salon will not be lost in their system, as they have a dedicated in-house salon division that tracks and examines the interchange rates specifically for thousands of salon businesses across the nation. Acquiring this data has enabled Integrity with the exceptional ability to verify that salon owners are being charged correctly and at the best rate for their specific business.

Does the Processor Understand the Salon Business?

Another indicator of an appropriate credit card processor for your business is how well the company understands the salon business and the challenges you face. If the credit card processor is endorsed by respected industry partners such as Redken, Pureology, L'Oreal Professional, Matrix, Mizani, and others, it is a good sign that they offer a mix of services and products which will be most appropriate for salon owners. Other endorsements to look for include the Summit Salon Business Center (the largest salon consulting firm), The Salon Professional Academy schools, State Beauty Supply, RDA ProMart distributor stores, and Salon Centric (the largest salon product distribution hub in America).

Beyond the endorsements of industry professionals, salon owners should be aware of additional programs and services tailored exclusively to the salon owner's business needs. For example, Integrity Payment Systems (which is endorsed by the above mentioned salon industry companies and more) has created four unique services to help create a successful and profitable salon. Salon owners control each of these products and direct each of the percentages, which include:

1. Auto-Save: a system which helps salon owners build an emergency fund automatically by separating a small percentage of each transaction into their savings account.

2. Pay-Fast Bill Payment: helps salon owners automatically stay current with bills by directing a percentage of each transaction to payment of key vendors.

3. Pay-Fast Debt Elimination: eliminates debt by systematically directing a portion of each transaction to pay creditors.

4. B.O.B. (Beauty Of Budgeting): helps salon owners accurately anticipate costs, revenue, and other budget items to plan for profitability.

Because salon owners are part of the Integrity team, the company was able to look at issues affecting owners and devise helpful solutions which leverage the credit card processing technology.

Better management of credit and debit processing can add new customers and increase the average ticket size. With the help of special tools, salon owners can save for the future, pay off debts, and budget for improved profitability.

CHAPTER 18

Choosing a Phone System for Your Salon

Small-business phone systems are available in a variety of configurations, offering an ever-growing range of features and benefits that will help you communicate more efficiently with your clients and staff. The days of running out and buying a phone are a thing of the past. Choosing the right phone system for your business today is a more daunting task.

The newest and most advanced technology best suited for your salon runs on an Internet Protocol (IP) network. The network can be used to connect your home, office, and employees' devices and information resources.

When evaluating what type of phone system and service to use, you will first need to decide what works in your salon environment, and how important it is for you to be able to reach certain key employees at work and while at home.

Understanding the Needs of Your Business

The right small-business phone system can give your staff the tools they need to be more efficient. Does the salon need the phone to ring on multiple devices? Is it important to be able to have your home office as an extension on the system? Is it necessary to have a phone in the dispensary area, salon office, or break room?

It's important to know what your salon needs so you can choose wisely among the many features offered. Many of the features may be overkill for your salon. With technology advancing at such a quick rate, the value of choosing the right system can make communicating with your staff so much easier. Some offer options that give you more flexibility and mobility and allow you to connect via your phone system from home or while on the road. Among the many features and capabilities to consider:

- Mobile softphones—for using your computer as a phone. Great for booking appointments.

- Videoconferencing—a great tool for having a meeting while out of town or having an education class.

- Paging and Intercom—wonderful tool for letting one of your team members know that their next client has arrived or that they have a phone call.

- Presence Technology—gives your front desk person the ability to see who is available at any given time, as well as the best way to reach them.

- Wireless IP Phones—enabling staff to access data and be easily accessible when in the break room or supply room.

- Unified messaging—providing notifications by email, text message, or voicemail. Great for keeping in touch with your salon, staff, and clients.

Cutting-Edge Technology

Your new small-business phone system can help your employees do things that once were not possible. It will change the way you do business. Being in touch enables you to make business decisions on the spot. You know when there is a problem and you can quickly connect to your key people in an instant. The benefits of using an IP system are listed below.

1. Your receptionist never has to leave his or her area to communicate with staff.

2. Messages can be forwarded directly to your mobile or home phone.

3. Messages can also be forwarded to your email.

4. Your staff does not have to leave a customer's side when they need to ask you a question.

5. You can set up a conference call with your entire staff, communicating in real time.

6. The system is wireless.

7. Studies have shown that by using an IP system, you will save up to 40 percent on your phone bill and up to 90 percent on international calls.

8. You can get reports and monitor calls on each line in your salon.

9. Flexibility when adding more users to your system.

10. All of your employees can be tied together.

The benefits of having the IP system in your new or remodeled salon will outweigh the older, traditional phone systems. You can now be connected to your business from anywhere in the world. Imagine that you are on vacation and staying at a hotel with a high-speed Internet connection. You can now receive and make calls through your softphone just like you were sitting in your salon. The person you are talking to will have no idea where you are calling from while conducting business.

Don't just improve the way you do business, you must explore technology and be open-minded to change. These new phone systems will allow you better time management, increased functionality, and improved productivity in your salon with a lower cost.

CHAPTER 19

Your Purpose, Your Name—Why Your Business Name Is Important

"What's in a name? That which we call a rose by any other name would smell as sweet."

—William Shakespeare

Selecting a name for your salon is not easy. A name reflects more than the identity of your company. It tells customers who you are, what you do, and more than a little about how you do it. Your customers should be able to get an idea of what to expect when they walk through your door. If you do it right, your name will differentiate you from your peers, pique your customers' interest, and invite further investigation.

What's in a name? A lot, when it comes to small business success. The right name can make your company the talk of the town—the wrong one can doom you into obscurity and failure. If you're smart, you will put as much effort into naming your salon as you did with coming up with the idea to open one. Ideally, your name should convey the expertise, value, and uniqueness of the products or services you plan to offer.

How you come up with a name is largely a matter of personal preference. Some people want to include their own name as part of their salon. Others may use the location of the salon or even something that reflects the history of the town or building. There are many different ways to choose names. We have come up with some effective elements that will help you with the process.

Tell Us Who You Are

Your name should reflect your identity. It is an essential aspect of branding. You will be promoting this name, getting it in front of as many eyes as possible, as often as possible. How do you want the public to think of you and your salon?

For some, that means integrating your name or the names of your children into your business. We don't recommend this because if you want to sell your salon in the future, the name is synonymous with you and you only. If you leave the business, the name dies when you leave. The potential buyer may and should view this as a big problem. It would be better to be known as the "Color Salon" than "Pat's Color Salon." People would view you as a full-service salon with expertise in hair color, instead of a one-person salon with expertise in hair color.

Tell Us What You Do

It is incredible how many business names give little, if any, indication of what services they actually provide. Try to choose a name that you want your salon to be identified with. If you're starting a salon that is for new, progressive hairstyles, you want a name that conveys fresh styles, innovation, talent, and fashion, something different, or out of this world. Doing so will also set the stage for new stylists who may be looking for a change of job and a fresh start. By letting your name tell prospective clients and employees what you do, your name will open doors you may never believe possible.

Just Another Salon

Your salon name is the first opportunity to tell customers how you are different from the competition. That can be done by emphasizing what makes you different, pinpointing what aspect of your products and services can't be found anywhere else, or what you do better than the salon down the street.

Pique Customers' Interest

Creating customer interest is an art and a science. Think carefully about your target market. What qualities of your services are of great importance to your customers? What type of words would appeal to that client? The words in your name should be inviting, approachable, and make customers feel like they will be comfortable in your place of business.

Let's Do It

What do you need to help you come up with a name? Find a quiet room, thesaurus, writing pad, some good feedback from family and friends. The process shouldn't take you more than a few hours. Here are some quick tips on getting started:

- Brainstorm: Think about how you want people to feel when they hear your name.
- Relate: Think about related words and phrases that evoke the feelings you want.
- Experiment: Start playing with combinations of various words and phrases or unique spellings for words.

- Reflect: Review your list and give some thought to each name and how you feel when you hear it.

- Communicate: Go over it with family and friends and have them give their gut feeling on what they think.

- Prioritize: Throw out the names you hate and only keep the ones you like.

- Check domain names: See if the name is available for a domain name on the Internet.

- Have fun: Remember that this name will be with you for a long time.

Salon Owner/Operators Discuss the Good, the Bad, & the Ugly

Diane Couto, Owner Operator of Valdemar Hair Studio

"Valdemar was my grandfather's first name. He was artistic in so many ways. For me, it was a sentimental choice and inspirational. I would never sell it; it's part of me and my culture . . . he is what I do!"

Lauren Cassidy, Owner/Operator of Visions For the Art of Hair

"I am a visionary and an artist of hair."

Cheri Shinn Blanca, Owner/Operator of Studio Tru

"I was being "Tru" to myself for doing what I love and believe in."

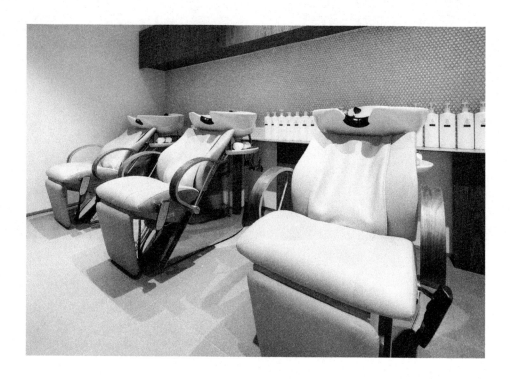

CHAPTER 20

Business Insurance—Why You Need It!

Business insurance protects you and your business from liability, accidents, or damage. Salon owners trying to save a few dollars when opening a salon make the crucial mistake of forgoing business insurance. Good luck and positive thinking will not protect you, your staff, and customers from losses. Unfortunately, bad things happen even to the most conscientious owners.

Factual Scenarios: This Can Happen To You

- You arrive at work to find your shampoo shuttle leaked all over your brand-new hardwood floors and the entire floor is buckled.

- A customer slips in your shampoo area and breaks her ankle.

- One of your customers has a heart attack while having her hair colored.

- One of your employees leaves the coffee maker on and it burns down your salon and building.

- A member of your staff cuts a customer while giving a haircut.

- One of your staff stains a very expensive wedding dress while preparing a bride for her wedding day.

- You suddenly need carpal tunnel surgery and will not be able to work for two months.

As you can see, there are many different reasons why you will need insurance for you and for your salon. Different types of insurance can cover the contents of your salon, your health, liability, and your property. Having insurance for everything can be quite expensive. Let's focus on what will suit your needs when first opening a salon.

Liability Insurance

What has the world come to? America was once known as the "promised land." A person could come and build a business empire from the ground up and have a fresh start. Nowhere else in the world could you do this like in the United States.

We are now known for something else. America is known for lawsuits. Lawsuits are like baseball, apple pie, and hamburgers—it's the American way. Let me add one more thing to the list—lawyers. You need to protect your business from legal expenses, settlements or judgments, and lawsuits. Liability policies cover business losses for payments to victims of bodily injury or property damage caused by your business. This insurance will also cover medical expenses to victims, attorney fees, and expenses associated with legal proceedings. General liability is a must-have for your daily business operation.

Business Property Insurance

Business property insurance covers your business in case of unforeseen damage or loss to your building, inventory, or equipment. That means even if the neon sign hanging out in front of your salon shorts out in a storm, you would be covered to have it fixed or replaced. Business property insurance coverage extends to items such as: laptops, phones, furniture, and valuable documents.

Types of Business Property Insurance

According to the National Association of Insurance Commissioners, there are three kinds of business property insurance:

1. **Basic**—covers damages from natural disasters such as fire, storms, and explosions.
2. **Broad**—covers the basic damages, plus other unforeseen events, such as a riot, that leaves the salon in shambles.
3. **Special**—the most comprehensive form of business insurance. It covers basic and broad, plus all the direct physical loss that is included in your policy.

Business Property Insurance for Owners Who Rent Their Store

If you rent your store, don't think the landlord is responsible for losses to your business and property. While the building itself is most likely covered, your inventory, computers, salon equipment, and other property related to your business are not. You must have business property insurance to cover the contents of your salon.

If you have financed your salon equipment, computers, phone system, or any other equipment, the bank or finance company will make it mandatory that you have personal property insurance on everything you financed through them.

Key Person Insurance

Most small businesses, and almost all start-up businesses, depend on the talents or abilities of a few key people. If you are a "one-man band" or rely on just a few people for the success of your business, your business could fail if something should happen to you or any of your key people. Key person insurance is a way for businesses to insure against business interruption if a key person becomes injured or ill.

Workers' Compensation Insurance

Workers' Compensation coverage is required by state, local, and federal law. If you have employees, you will have no choice about it. The fact of the matter is, if one of your employees gets hurt at work, whether it's your fault or not, you want to be prepared for a lawsuit. Workers' Compensation Insurance will cover hospital bills, attorney fees, lawsuit awards, and lost wages.

Buying Insurance

Start by finding three insurance companies in your area. Explain exactly what kind of business you will be opening and how many employees you will have. You also need to have a list of the contents (equipment) that will be used in your place of business. Explain to the agent or broker what types of services you will offer. They may feel you need additional coverage. There are a few variables to consider when purchasing your insurance: price, coverage offered, specialization of insurance company, reputation of the insurance company, and the size of the deductible.

Price

Settling on the lowest price is not always the best choice. If one company is much cheaper than another, they may be leaving out a large portion of your coverage. Ask questions, read the policies, and compare.

Coverage

Negotiate more coverage in all aspects. No policy is cast in stone. The worst they can say is no. When it comes to insurance, it doesn't hurt to be over-insured.

Specialization of the Company

Each industry and business has its own risk. When picking an insurance company, make sure they specialize in small businesses and have insured other salons.

Reputation of the Insurance Company

Try to work with an insurance company in your area. They may be on "Main Street" in your town. It also makes sense to look online to see if they are in good financial shape.

You can check with "Best Insurance Reports." If the company is not rated from an A+ to a B, you should look elsewhere for your insurance.

Deductible

The deductible is one of the most important parts of your policy. A higher deductible will mean lower insurance costs, but it will also increase how much you have to pay for any losses you may have.

Whatever you do, remember that whoever is writing your insurance policies is doing so because he or she earns commissions on these policies. Your interests and theirs may not always agree. It means that you should shop around, negotiate, and always be on the lookout for a better deal.

As a business owner, you know the value of protecting yourself, your family, and your staff and customers. Be sure to purchase an insurance policy that will safeguard all aspects of your investment.

Salon Owner/Operators Discuss the Good, the Bad, & the Ugly

Marissa's House of Style

"We had a fire in the salon. Most of the salon was destroyed. I had the right insurance company. A client's husband was my insurance agent. He guided me through the whole crisis. I was able to rebuild my salon from the ground up. My salon is now more beautiful than before. Thank the Lord I had the right insurance. I was blessed."

CHAPTER 21

The Color of Money—What Color Is Your Business?

"It's a good thing God created the rainbow and didn't consult an interior decorator or he would still be looking at swatches and picking colors."

—Sam Levenson

As a salon owner, you have a meaningful understanding of the color of money, but how about the color of your business? You must understand what colors you choose in your business puts your customers in a buying mood or creates the wrong perception of your salon.

You may have never thought that there is a science of colors. Colors have an impact on our body and mind. Big corporate businesses have been studying and using colors to influence buyers for many years. Market research specialists have applied their knowledge to many businesses around the world to help business owners leverage every angle to enhance retail buying. Color is often called the "silent salesperson." Color must immediately attract the holder's eye, convey the message of what the business is about, create a brand identity, and most importantly, help make the sale.

The power of colors stimulates our nervous system and evokes emotional states. The colors of the environment trigger feelings to the brain, causing various hormonal releases. You may be thinking, "Wow, this all seems crazy, too much information, brain overload, is this really important?" Yes, it sure is. Let's forget the science and find out why the right colors will show you the "green" (money) in your salon.

The Meaning of Colors & Your Business

The meaning of colors varies depending on one's culture, race, gender, and even age. It's not just the selection of colors in general, but also which colors to use with your target customer. Much of the human reaction to color is subliminal and customers in your salon will generally not be aware of the persuasive effects of color.

We have listed the colors below that have emotional connections between people and certain colors or color patterns.

Reinvent the Color Wheel to Your Advantage

White: Pure, clean, youthful. White is a neutral color that can imply purity in fashion, cleanliness, peace, innocence, winter, snow, and marriage.

Black: Power, elegance, secretive, sexy. The color black can target your heightened market or be used in youth marketing to "add sexy" to your look and image.

Red: Passion, excitement, danger, strength, speed. Red is the color of attention, causing the blood pressure and heart rate to rise. Use red to inject excitement into your salon or brand.

Orange: Vibrant, energy, playful. Add some fun to your company by creating a playful environment for your customers.

Yellow: Happy, warm, alert. Yellow can be an attractor for your business retail area by promoting a relaxing feeling.

Green: Natural, healthy, plentiful. To create a calming effect or growth image, choose green. Go green, go!

Blue: Loyal, peaceful, and trustworthy. Blue is the most popular and neutral color on a global scale. It is a safe choice for a salon in building customer loyalty.

When deciding your color choice for the salon, remember that colors have meaning. The customers you attract may depend on the colors you choose. Is your salon located in an older or younger market? Is your salon near a college or retirement community, or is the area in a hip part of town? All this will help you choose what colors best fit your market and customer base.

When choosing the colors in your salon, think about the following:

○ Impulse shoppers are attracted and go toward reds, oranges, blacks, or blues.

○ If you are trying to attract people who plan ahead when purchasing, then lean toward pink, light blue, or navy.

○ If you are in a higher income area, where status is everything to your customers, you may want to think about more classic and subtle colors.

○ If you are in a middle class area, you should look at bright colors for your retail area.

○ If you live in a hot climate or close to the beach, your customer will welcome brighter colors in your salon.

○ If you live in a colder climate, your clients will prefer neutral, more traditional colors.

Salon Owner/Operators Discuss the Good, the Bad, & the Ugly

Impulse Salon, Atlanta

"We are in a high-end area inside a beautiful strip mall. The area attracts very wealthy clients. We knew we had to do something special when decorating and picking colors. We have subtle colors throughout the salon. The entrance hall of the salon was done in light beige leather wallpaper with beautiful rich moldings. The retail area was also done the same way. Our clients love it! And, yes, we do well with retail."

CHAPTER 22

The Importance of Signage

Signage in front or on top of your storefront is your billboard. Your sign is the single most effective way to communicate what your business is, what you do, what you sell, and what you offer. Business signage is a representation of you and your business.

Customers attracted by business signage include those who are just passing by or those who are new to the neighborhood. A sign is the most effective way to reach this group of potential customers.

If your business site is in an area that is not easily accessible, then your sign is the only thing that can communicate to people who are driving by your salon. The salon located off a freeway can use a high-rise sign to attract some of the people traveling on nearby roads and expressways.

Signage—A Way of Life

Ever since anyone can remember, signs have been used as an effective marketing tool for different occasions, events, and business purposes. From the moment you leave your house, you will see one sign or another within five minutes. It makes you wonder why we don't get information overload from signage. There is a reason why some signs have impact on you and others just blend in with the environment. Sign overload is a way of life, but making a sign with a lasting impact on the customer should be your goal. Your sign must effectively touch the emotion and life of your customer.

All Shapes, Sizes, & Designs

The big question you are going to have is what type of sign do you put on your location and what material should you use? They can range from PVC, neon, or steel/aluminum. Signage designs can suit a variety of budget, design, landlord, and city requirements.

Remember, business signage does not have to be just metal or large neon. You can utilize all kinds of modern technologies and inventions such as:

- Plastics that do not rust, where you can interchange graphics as products and/or models change for haircare products.
- Weatherproof digital banner signs that go on your personal car or store windows.

When designing your sign, it must be easy to read and placed where it can be easily seen.

City or Town Requirements & Costs

Each city or town will have different requirements and restrictions, such as: height, placement, colors, or material. Your city or town may not allow signs in the windows and/or obstructions on the lawn in front of your location. To find out what is acceptable, contact your local building department and request the current guidelines.

The cost of your signs will vary depending on what product the sign is made out of and if it is illuminated. The least expensive sign is aluminum and steel, ranging from $2000 to $4000. An illuminated block letter sign will range from $3000 to $7000, depending on the size and number of letters. Graphics for your store windows will depend on the size and layout and how many colors, but will range between $500 and $1000. Weatherproof sign graphics for your car will cost between $1000 for half of your car and $2000 for a full-size car or van.

> **NOTE**
>
> The landlord may want you follow the same design as everyone else in the plaza. Read your lease carefully for the requirements and restrictions, such as size and type, and whether window signs and neon are allowed.

When deciding upon the type of sign or where you will place it, have you thought about these very important items?

Check off the questions below as you answer them.

○ Will your sign be visible from all directions?

○ Will your sign attract new customers?

○ Will your sign "brand" your salon?

○ Is your sign appealing and legible?

○ Can you put your logo on the sign?

○ Does it need to be illuminated?

○ Will it block your windows?

○ Is there any obstruction or part of the building that limits its size?

CHAPTER 23

Startup Expense Worksheet

Below is a breakdown of expenses you may incur. If they do not apply, leave them blank.

Item and Area	Expense
Construction	
Permits	
Impact Fees (from the city)	
Architect Plans	
Designer	
Rent (first, last, and security deposit)	
Salon Furniture	
Salon Front Desk Computer	
a. software program	
b. copier/printer	
Office Furniture	
a. desk and chair	

(Spreadsheet is continued on next page)

(Spreadsheet is continued from previous page)

Item and Area	Expense
b. computer	
c. copier/printer	
Business License (city and state)	
a. Lawyer	
b. Accountant	
Business Insurance	
Utility Deposits	
a. water	
b. electric	
c. telephone/Internet service	
d. garbage (may be included with location)	
Advertising	
a. website	
b. social marketing	
c. magazines	
d. city or county contributions	
e. Web hosting or domain name	
Initial Retail and Salon Supplies	
MISC. Expenses (approx. 7%)	
TOTAL	

CHAPTER 24

The Money Hunt

"The lack of money is the root of all evil."

—Mark Twain

Where to Find Business Startup Money

When it comes to financing these days, it is more difficult than ever to find a bank that has the resources and willingness to lend to a small business. Given certain economic conditions, achieving the American Dream and one day owning your own salon may prove to be extremely difficult. You may have all the skills, education, drive, and personality, but lack one very important aspect—money!

The money factor puts limitations on any new business venture and destroys dreams. If you are lucky enough to either borrow from family members or have your own personal savings, that's great. But, these options can put you in a compromising position.

If opening your own salon is your dream, don't be discouraged. Financial alternatives can assist you in not only making this a reality, but a success.

How Deep Are Your Pockets?

The idea of financing your new business may be scary at first glance, but it's the most popular source of business startup money. First, look at what you have available and what you could easily liquidate:

- How much cash do you have in your bank accounts?
- What assets can you sell? (Cars, jewelry—gold and silver are at all-time highs—and antiques)
- Do you have a stock portfolio that you can leverage?
- Can you draw equity from real estate or a home that you own?

Family & Friends

The second most popular source of business startup money is from family and friends. They may be willing to provide a business startup loan or an outright gift due to the fact they believe in you and your business plan. The advantages of a personal loan or gift are that it eliminates the bank paperwork, credit approval process, and bank fees. A major drawback is that if the business falters your relationship with family or friends may not survive. It will certainly cause tension and negativity at the next family function.

Credit Cards

A recent study stated that over 54 percent of businesses use credit cards in some capacity to get up and running. Credit cards provide instant money, and you can deduct the interest you pay if what you purchase is a business expense. Remember, easy money is harder to pay back. Most credit card money is lent at about 15 to 19 percent. Opening a business with this type of money can put you in a downward tailspin with no way out.

Life Insurance Policy

If you hold a whole life insurance policy with at least three years of maturity, you can likely get a loan against the cash value of your policy. Most insurance companies will lend you up to 90 percent of your policy's cash value at rates generally more attractive than those charged by credit card companies. You must continue to keep up with your premium payments on your policy.

Retirement Plan

Still working for a salon while starting a business? Then, check into borrowing against your 401(k). While rules vary, you can generally borrow half of what you have put into your retirement plan, up to a maximum of $50,000. The drawback is that when taking out the money, you will be penalized 10 percent and you will have to pay the taxes on the amount you take out of the 401(k).

Finding Funding on the Web

The Internet has changed how business startups find new business funding. Numerous sites on the Web offer advice about how to put together a business plan and connect you with various sources that can help you find the money needed to go forward with your business plan.

Here are some reference sites:

- **www.bizoffice.com**
- **www.businessfinance.com**
- **www.fundingpost.com**

The sites listed allow you to search for funding sources and access business guidelines. These sites will navigate you through a step-by-step guide to creating, supporting, and presenting your funding request.

Bank Loans

Bank loans are tough for any new startups to acquire. Usually, banks loan money to companies that are stable and profitable and that have been in business more than three years. Banks will also look for owners who have a proven track record and business background. Loans from banks are not impossible to obtain, but the requirements these days are far more difficult. We will discuss the approval procedure later in this chapter.

SBA Financing

Depending on your credit record and the strength of your business plan, you may be able to secure a Small Business Administration (SBA) loan. An SBA loan is guaranteed by the government and usually has a better interest rate than a conventional bank loan. Most bank loans are five year, whereas SBA loans can be as long as ten years. The longer payback term is helpful to a new business venture and certainly takes the burden off of paying back the loan over a shorter period. It will make the first few years of business much easier to not have a large loan payment every month. The downside of working with the SBA is that the application process is very tedious, the completion process intense, and the approval process can take up to 6 months before you get a response on your loan status.

More recently, SBA loans for $5000 to $50,000 have become available that provide an approval process of less than two weeks.

- **www.strategiesforsmallbusiness.com**
- **www.sba.gov**

Home Equity

If you own your home, you can take out a home equity loan, a second mortgage, or refinance your original mortgage. You can borrow as much as 80 percent of your home's equity. The most important thing to remember when you borrow against your home is, if your business should fail, the bank will foreclose on your home unless you have the means to pay it back. (This option is discussed in detail later in the chapter.)

Leasing

Leasing sources can accommodate all applicants for financing whether you are in business 20 years or a new startup salon. Leasing programs give you the flexibility to finance your furniture, equipment, and installation. The application is less tedious than working with conventional banks. Once you fill out a lease application, you should have an answer within

72 hours. The bank also does not put liens on your house or other assets. If you have been declined by a bank, you may find it worthwhile to try a lease company.

- Quest Resources
- Castleton Capital

Government-Related Startup Programs

Many government operated organizations promote economic development and provide assistance to help particular types of people succeed in business. Often, this assistance includes financial support, such as startup business loans. Each state has programs that may be beneficial in a startup business. There are also many women's organizations throughout the country that assist women who are trying to open a business.

Partnership

Partners can be a great source of financing support for a startup salon business. You will have additional capital as well as benefit from the skills and experience another individual brings to your business. A partnership may include financial support or being able to share responsibilities of running the day-to-day operations of the business. Conversely, you will have to share profits, and if the business does not work out, you will have to terminate your partnership and most likely your friendship.

Money is an important aspect for your business to succeed. Being able to obtain it without the restrictions of giving up your business or putting your house up as collateral is not going to be an easy task. Obtaining money with high interest rates will not make it easy for you in the early stages of opening a business.

How to Get a "YES" From Your Banker

Proper preparation and knowing the correct answers to the most common banking questions often determines whether your bank gives you a yes or a no answer when you apply for a loan. The best way to prepare is to be ready to answer all objections.

Bankers most commonly reject a loan for one of five reasons. However, it is possible to overcome them and get approved if you follow the suggestions in the next section.

1. No sound business plan
2. Not knowing the exact amount of money you need and what it will be used for
3. Not showing the ability to pay back the loan
4. Poor credit worthiness
5. Little to no money in the bank

Effectively Informing the Bank About You & Your Business

Take these key steps to ensure that the loan officer is properly informed.

1. Put together a sound business plan. The plan can be a few pages, but it should be well thought out. The business plan shows the loan officer you have credibility as the owner and that you're not just rushing into something you are uncertain of.

2. Be prepared to supply business credit references and your personal credit history. The applicant must have a proven track record in repaying distributors and suppliers. It is also important that all personal obligations (mortgages, car loans, student loans, and credit cards) be paid in a timely manner. If you have a history of slow payment on any of these, you must have a sufficient explanation in writing or your loan request will be immediately denied. Good personal and business credit policies are the keys to success!

3. Provide a brief description of the beauty industry, including the average and top salaries of stylists, and the projected annual revenue for your salon business. Use industry magazines and special publications, such as Salon Today's Top 200. Remember, most bankers are unaware that our industry has grown into a multibillion dollar profession. The bank has to feel confident that the beauty industry is professional and has the potential for growth. Unfortunately, the reputation of our industry has been tarnished by individuals who have not run their business on a professional level. But, the beauty industry has come a long way in 10 years. Therefore, educate your banker on how profitable the beauty industry has become.

4. Share your education and experience in running a business and your support structure. If you've taken classes at a local college, get letters of recommendation from your instructors. Show the bank your performance record in school. If you have held a management position in a salon, provide them with a letter of recommendation and share how you improved the performance of the salon during your term in the management position. If you can, put together an advisory board of people you know who are willing to help you get your business off the ground. Most of us know people in marketing, business management, accounting, etc., and they may be willing to meet with you as a favor to give you free advice.

State Why You Need the Money

When a loan officer asks you how much money you need to borrow, don't reply with, "How much will you loan me?" While preparing for your loan, conduct an in-depth analysis of your borrowing needs and stipulate whether you're starting a new business or remodeling/expanding an existing business. You must have all of your costs outlined and on paper before going to a loan officer. The worksheet in Chapter 23 will be helpful. By creating a business plan, you should get an idea of how much operating capital you will need in order to open and operate throughout the early months.

Do Your Numbers Support the Loan Request?

If your business has been at a break-even point, or even losing money, there's still hope. However, it won't be easy. Bankers are trained to make decisions based primarily on a company's ability to generate sufficient cash flow through consistent profitability. If you have lost money, you need to know the reason for the loss. The loss may be caused by the economy, poor health, labor problems, or the weather! Hurricane Katrina is an example of this. Banks understood the unforeseen catastrophe and modified many loans. The bank will want to know what changes the owner will make to fix these problems, if possible.

The most important thing the bank is looking for is the income and profit you are reporting on your tax returns. Remember, hiding income from Uncle Sam when filing your taxes will only hurt you when applying for a business loan. Also, keep in mind loan officers never want to hear, "My tax return doesn't reflect what I actually make." Such a statement will not give the right impression and not reporting income is illegal. It will guarantee a decline.

What Type of Collateral Do You Have?

Small business owners complain that lenders lack an adequate understanding of the market value of assets such as furniture, equipment, and inventory (supplies). And, they are right! Bankers aren't experts on most of the collateral given, no matter what is being pledged. Banks will generally lend no more than 80 percent of the value of real estate/equipment.

You may have personal assets, such as debt-free automobiles, bank certificates, stocks, or real estate that could be used to secure the loan. It is guaranteed the bank will ask you to secure your entire business and will usually look for other avenues outside the business, as well as personal assets, for collateral. You must address these issues before applying for your loan. An unsecured loan is almost impossible in today's banking world.

Personal Guarantee(s)

Most banks won't lend to any business without personal guarantees from the owner(s). The purpose of a guarantee is to provide a secondary repayment source for the loan in the event the small business is unable to pay. What this means is, if you borrow $10,000 and default on the loan, the bank will go after you, personally, for the remaining loan. If you don't have the money, they have the right to seize any personal assets that equal the amount of the loan.

As a matter of policy, banks ask for personal guarantees from the owner(s). The guarantee demonstrates a full commitment on your part, which will enhance your chances for loan approval.

Applying for a small business loan is not an easy process. Banks are not in the business to lose money; that's why their procedures have become so arduous. They do not want any risky propositions. However, if you are prepared to answer these common inquiries from bankers, you will improve your chances of obtaining the financing you need.

Good preparation and showing confidence in your ideas as an owner will help establish the credibility necessary to convince the banker you have business smarts and what it takes to run a business.

Using Your Home as Collateral

Most first-time business owners are so sure they will succeed in their business, some are willing to put up their biggest asset as collateral: Their Home Sweet Home!

Banks, by nature, are very conservative. Now more than ever, they are extremely cautious when lending money, especially for a new business. They feel the risk is so high for a new business that they will ask you for personal assets such as a pledged 401(k), life insurance policy, bank certificates, stocks, or any debt-free real estate to secure a startup business loan, not to mention the personal guarantee of every person involved with the business.

If you are considering pledging your home as collateral, be aware of what could happen if your business should fail. We are sure the worst feeling in the world would be for you to receive a phone call letting you know that your home is now being seized because you pledged it as collateral for your new business loan. The other way the bank will notify you is when the local sheriff comes and stops by your house with a warrant letting you know that your house is being seized because of default on your loan payments. It is not a game and should not be taken lightly.

Generally, banks try to negotiate a new payment plan when they see your business is in trouble. This will allow you to pay the debt back gradually, without being asked to leave your home. The bank's position, as far as personal residences and businesses go, is to try and work with the borrower or guarantor as much as possible. Banks look at homes as a last resort. They are not in the real estate business nor do they want to be. Banks do not want to retain assets, especially residential real estate. But, you must be realistic. You pledged your home as collateral, and if you are forced to close your business, they will take your home. Beware of the consequences!

Currently, the value of business assets amounts to 10 to 20 cents on the dollar when auctioned off. After the entire salon is auctioned off, the bank will look to the borrowers to find a way to settle the remaining debt. At this point, you will wish you never opened your business and pledged your home.

When a bank accepts a home as collateral on a startup business loan, they put a lien on the home for the entire value of the loan amount borrowed, even if the debt is more than the homeowner's equity. The bank's philosophy is that in time, the equity will increase through appreciation of the home over the length of the business loan. The bank's lien will be a secondary lien behind the primary mortgage holder.

If the business should fail, it doesn't necessarily mean that the home has to be sold to settle your debt or that you will be evicted from your home. If the homeowner has enough equity, then you can refinance the mortgage, use this equity to pay off the balance of the business loan with the bank, and get the lien removed and keep your home.

The people whose businesses fail and don't have enough equity in their homes, or have additional debt, may opt for personal bankruptcy. Typically, this allows the borrower to work out a repayment plan and avoid losing his home to satisfy creditors.

Bankruptcy is actually the most common course of action borrowers take. They try just about anything to save their business and home. They will borrow from family members, run up credit card debt, and borrow against virtually every other asset they have.

At this point, they have usually defaulted on their business loan, incurred significant debt from vendors, credit cards, and state/federal taxes. It's not just the bank that has not been paid, but a whole barrage of creditors. When this happens, it is hopeless to continue the business.

Most banks speak to the business owners on a regular basis. In most cases, the borrower is required to give an annual update on the business with their tax returns. The key is to have open communications with your bank. If you see that you are having difficulties with the business, notify the bank as early as possible. A monthly visit with your accountant will also help you with bookkeeping and keep your business records up to date and on time. It is better to be proactive with your bank when you see that you're having financial difficulty.

Going into business has great rewards, this is true. However, not all of us are always so fortunate. Remember, putting up your home should be your very last resort. Never give what can't be given back.

Leasing for the Life of Your Business

Most entrepreneurs start businesses with sweat equity and their savings. In many cases, the salon owner runs short of monies due to cost overruns. It seems like Murphy's Law always strikes halfway through the project. Your architect or interior designer informs you that the electrical system isn't adequate or the plumbing is too old to fix, or the city is requiring a one-time impact fee for water.

The total cost of your project is now over budget $10,000 to $15,000, and you still haven't ordered your sign. If your local bank did not approve your loan, then leasing may be an alternative.

Distributors and manufacturers in the beauty industry have been aware of these bank hang-ups and explored other financing options to help their potential customers obtain the money to purchase their salon furniture. They found that furniture and equipment leasing was the answer.

Listed below are ten reasons why salon owners should use leasing as a financing tool, as opposed to conventional bank financing.

Bank vs. Lease Finance Company

In order to get approved at your local bank, the applicant must submit three years of personal and corporate tax returns with a completed application. The corporate returns must show a profit in order for the bank to even consider lending you any money. Leasing companies require that you fill out an application. That application is usually reviewed the same day it is submitted and can be approved up to $75,000. The process is quite different from the tedious bank loan application process. It's a fact that over 90 percent of salons would not qualify for the conventional bank loan in today's business environment because most salons fail to show profits. Good personal credit is the driving force for obtaining an approval.

Startup Financing

Most banks may not consider extending credit if your salon does not have a minimum of two years in business. Typically, the only lenders who will supply financing to startup salon businesses are those with a niche expertise in a particular line of equipment or industry. Therefore, if you are a new business owner, leasing may be your best and most competitive option for obtaining your new furniture and equipment. Your furniture and equipment salesperson will be able to point you in the right direction.

Establish Business Credit

Equipment lease financing is the perfect way to establish business credit if you are a new or existing salon. As your business grows, you will need to either trade up or acquire new furniture and equipment to meet your increased demand. By establishing your credit with a lease company, it will be easier to purchase your next piece of furniture or equipment or expand, relocate, or remodel your salon.

Home vs. Equipment

The only collateral pledged on an equipment lease is the equipment you are purchasing. The lease finance company will not ask for any other items to be pledged, such as a major asset or your personal residence, building, car, or your business itself. Conversely, it is nearly impossible to get a business loan from your neighborhood bank without pledging your home or a major asset as collateral.

Quick Turnaround

If opening your business or your remodel project is like most, you will run over budget and exhaust your cash supply before you have everything you need to open or reopen. Equipment lease financing allows you to avoid a lengthy approval process so that you can get your furniture and equipment ordered and installed within just a few weeks. Upon receipt of your credit application and equipment quotation, you can expect a rapid response and approval within 24 hours.

Conserve Your Money

Lease financing allows you to conserve your money, which you can utilize elsewhere in your business. Leasing is a predictable budgetary tool since payments are fixed and not subject to the fluctuations of a business loan that may go up with an increase in interest rates.

Down Payment

Equipment lease financing does not require a large down payment, which is the normal case with bank loans. You can expect to put down 10 percent or less of the equipment lease as a security deposit.

> **NOTE**
>
> All bank loan payments fluctuate monthly. Your monthly lease payment will always be the same.

Tax Advantages

Leasing offers the ability to write off your lease payments. Depending on your lease option, you may be able to subtract your lease payment as an expense every month for the term of the lease. A bank loan does not offer this write-off. Take advantage of the recently modified IRS Section 179 enabling businesses to write off thousands of dollars of leased equipment per year.

Avoid Obsolescence

Technology and designs are always changing, including new equipment for processing color, display cases, and salon software. Why should you be stuck with old and dated equipment? They can put your salon at a competitive disadvantage. Equipment financing allows you to receive the benefit of new equipment and technology today, while paying for it with tomorrow's dollars.

Going Out of Business

In the event of default, the lease agreement usually indicates that the lessor will repossess the leased equipment and resell it for its fair market value. It is very different from a bank loan, because if you default on your loan, the bank would have no interest in the equipment or reselling it on your behalf. However, the entire outstanding balance will be due and the asset pledged (such as your home) can be seized.

Today, there are only a handful of lease companies (mentioned previously) that focus on your niche—the beauty industry. You may find it easier to discuss your needs with a lease company who constantly works with the equipment manufacturer or distributor from whom you are buying your equipment. The process will enable you to work with a company who has a true understanding of the beauty industry, as well as your needs regarding the equipment you are purchasing and the cost to install it.

> Salon Owner/Operators Discuss the Good, the Bad, & the Ugly

Shannon Perry-Rawls

"Holding myself back from investing. Being scared to spend money. Being [too] frugal."

DeAnne Vaughan

"Making sure I had enough capital. Getting [too] busy with build-out, ordering product, etc. You need to have some in reserve and have an estimated spending plan. I also think start small and then build bigger."

Diane M. Fedrizzi

"Working capital. You have to make sure you have money stashed for emergencies. If there is a slow week, you need to have back-up for bills, supplies, loan payments, etc."

Judy Rice

"Despite opening Goldwaves salon in Fort Worth in 1988 and having a personal history of salon experience as a stylist, I still did not understand the daunting task of growing a business from very little capital. Mostly, I was under-capitalized and not clear of all the government quarterly tax filings and paperwork. I never got in trouble, but paid a few late penalties."

CHAPTER 25

Choosing Beauty Products to Sell

Choosing products for your salon to display and sell will be an important decision to make when starting your salon. Selling retail in your salon is another business in and of itself that is housed within your salon. The choices you make about which products to sell is extremely important. The options are limitless and the task may be overwhelming. Not only should there be a demand for your products, but it must be profitable and something you and your staff enjoy selling. Before you commit to a product line, consider the following factors:

Marketability

In today's retail world, finding and picking the right products to sell to your customers is the key to success. You and your clients see so many brands on television, in magazines, and on the Internet. What works better or is more marketable?

If you pick the wrong products, your customers won't buy them. If products are priced too high or aren't meeting current trends, you could be stuck with a ton of inventory and very little sales. Before considering what products to sell, determine your market and your clientele. Once you know what kind of customer and the desired market to target, choosing the right brands will be much easier.

Next, investigate the products that sell in your area. Inspect and visit other salons as a customer. However, do not fall for the pretense that if every salon in the area has a product, it must be good—that is not always the case. It's good to be different. If you don't like the look, smell, or feel of the products you are thinking about providing, it will be difficult for you to market and sell them to your clients. It's essential that the brands you choose to carry match with your target—your market clientele. Some of your customers will buy high-priced products; others may buy only low- or mid-priced products. The key is to provide a selection that appeals to a large population of your clientele.

Education & Training

Choosing a long-standing manufacturer that supports your salon with marketing materials, education, and training will position you and your staff for increased sales. Education is key! You must know all the features and benefits of the entire product line and learn the best ways to showcase the product to your clients.

Manufacturers may offer educational events in your salon on new products; and they will promote your salon on their website. They have trained consultants and business partners to assist with education from the front of your salon to the back. These consultants and partners can help guide you with business decisions. These are all key items that you may not have been aware of when deciding on a product line to carry. Don't think small business, think big. Aligning yourself and your salon with a big name can make or break your retail business.

Profit Margin

Selling expensive beauty products is usually more profitable, but can require more credibility to sell. When you are pricing your retail goods, there is a lot you have to keep in mind in order to turn a profit. You'll need to consider the direct and indirect costs that have to be added to the price of each item you sell. You must remember all the overhead expenses you have in the salon before establishing a price point. Also, don't forget about commissions to your employees. The best-selling products in your salon will never earn a profit if your margins are too small. Your manufacturer's representative should be able to assist you with pricing in order for you to maintain the correct profits.

Consumable Items

The best thing about selling beauty products are the recurring sales. We have seen many salons selling other items, such as jewelry and handbags. Those items take up very expensive space in your retail area. A consumable item that needs to be replaced on a regular basis, such as shampoos, sprays, and conditioners is a great way to establish long-term sales. By establishing a customer base with recurring products, customers will continue to come back to you again and again. When your client picks up that bottle of shampoo at home and it is empty, they will immediately think of where they got it and who sold it to them. That bottle of shampoo is a daily reminder of you and your salon.

What's Hot & What's Not

When it comes to selecting your brands, you need to see what's hot in the industry. Beauty trade magazines and industry trade shows will give you a good education on what's hot and what's not. Have a staff meeting. You may have some students joining your team. They should know the new products that have been introduced in their school and may have a better indication of what products are being used these days.

Competition

It is good and healthy to have competition and you can outsell them in retail if you market and display your products well. The location of your products in your salon is very important. Hiding product under a counter or behind your reception desk or locked in a cabinet will not help you sell product. To your clients, that means "do not touch" and it is ineffective.

Retail must be on display as soon as you walk in your salon. The customer must feel at home in your retail area. Make buying your products fun and have items that everyone can afford. Beautiful display cases, easy access, and educated staff will ensure that you sell more products than your competition. Have your staff talk about the products they use. You want your customers to go home with something. Manufacturers have small sample bottles or teaser items. Having products like this will allow your customers to try your products and come back and buy the next time.

Diversity

Keep your product offerings simple in the early stages of your opening. If your product line is narrow and focused, then your marketing efforts can be just as tightly focused, which will bring you the best results for your marketing dollars. As your business grows, so can your product line, as long as you keep new products compatible with your customers, location, and your market.

The most important thing you should ask yourself is, "Would I give this product to my best friend or use it myself?"

CHAPTER 26

Salon Menu Designed for Profit

Your salon menu is one of the most important aspects of your salon business. The menu must be treated as an investment and put together as a showpiece of your salon. The menu will represent all of your products, services, and salon culture. Its intent is to lure your new and existing clients into spending their money on several services and products based on their enticing descriptions.

Your salon menu should be an open invitation for ultimate pleasure and style. Give your clients the choice to spend on services and products they are able to access and understand with a price point they can afford.

The menu should solve the challenge of varied desires and budgets. By presenting a variety of services and products within price ranges all of your clients can afford, you give your clientele variety and the choice to buy a service and products with an understanding of exactly how much they will be spending.

The salon menu gives the client a sense of who you are, what you represent, and what you can do for them. The client must feel that you are offering an ultimate experience that no other salon can compare—with the highest level of quality. They must be convinced that your level of expertise is truly what you are portraying in your salon menu.

Listed below are items that will assist you with your menu design, price point, and layout:

Professional Designers

If you want a professional look, then hire a professional. A local printing company should be able to recommend a graphic artist to assist you with the design and layout of your menu. Ask to see the artist's portfolio so you can compare ideas on how you want your menu to look.

They will help you with the entire process from design, logo, layout, colors, and printing, as well as Web design.

Cover & Logo

The cover is the first thing the customer sees. Your logo should be front and center. You also need to include the salon name, address, phone number, Web address, and email address. Include information about online bookings and gift card purchases. Don't forget to include how clients can connect to you socially. The information should be easily identified and not in small print.

Shape, Size, & Color

The standard size menu is 8½" by 11" folded in half or a trifold, but depends on the amount of information you need to lay out. The piece should not be complicated.

Menus & Real Estate

When building your menu, you must be open-minded and look at it as a fine piece of real estate. Every item on your menu is a tenant who is renting space. Part of your job is to allocate the right space for the right tenant. Certain spots on the menu draw more attention than others. Upper right, left, and center on a trifold design, for example, is considered the high-rent district. Since those areas are the best real estate on the block, put the services and products that you would like to promote the most in those locations. Also, the most effort should go into these places for both images and text.

Who Designs the Services?

When deciding on services, you should involve your staff. The stylists are the ones who know what is cutting-edge and what is new in the industry. Why go through the process of trial and error when your staff is better suited to help you decide on services?

You should also have input from all your product sales representatives so they can assist with your decision making on what services and products, from their experience, are more profitable than others. It is very important because they are out on the road every day and see the trends of what makes money and what doesn't. Continually utilize their expertise. Ultimately, this will make your salon more profitable.

Trade shows and ongoing education should be mandatory. Education will give your salon and staff the cutting-edge in the industry for your area. You always want to be a leader in new trends, not a follower. Education is the cornerstone to standing out from the rest. It will also allow you to make changes on your menu, if necessary, if you see a new service that may be profitable. Listen to your clients—ask them what services or products they would like to see offered.

Your menu must carry the basic treatments and services, but you must revisit your menu at least once a year to see what is "hot" and what is "not." Then, make changes accordingly.

Menu & website

The salon menu should be cohesive with your website. A coordinated look is very important with your branding of the salon. The colors, pictures, and pricing should match your menu, advertising, and business cards. Your message or mission statement should also be posted on the menu, business cards, and website.

Since product lines and services may change in your salon, it is a good idea to direct guests to your website for more specific details. Doing so will allow you to extend the lifetime of the printed menus. You may find that clients use your online menu rather than your print menu, saving you time and money on reprinting. You may only need to reprint when you run out.

Focus on Your Stars

Designing your menu around your team is essential. We're sure you have done your homework when hiring and have some very talented stylists. Make sure you choose your headliners and build your menu around them accordingly. If you have a strong color team, your menu should emphasize that strength. Your salon should be known as a progressive styling salon and your menu should advertise this aspect. Focusing on your stars allows you to build a winning team based on their strengths; a successful salon should not be built on the talents of one individual, but on the entire team.

Pricing

Correct pricing is essential for the success of your business. It has to be established from the first day you open. Your salon can get rave reviews and your services can be perfect; however, if your pricing is too expensive, you will wipe out any good reviews your salon has generated. You can have the best stylists and colorists in town, but people may not come back if they feel violated by your pricing. It is tricky and a sensitive subject.

Establishing price points is merely doing your homework. Check other salon/spa websites in your immediate area and actual menu pricing. Speak to your sales representatives or product distributors who can give you an idea of average pricing. Finally, get to know your clients and the areas where they live and work. You should be able to establish the correct pricing to meet the current market and location of your salon. People want value for their money, but that doesn't mean that you have to be the lowest price in town. If a customer perceives that they got more than what they paid for, then you have delivered service and product at a value. You need to offer both value and service and this should be reflected in your pricing.

Costs & How Much to Print

Printing the right amount has always been a guessing game. You would love to have enough business that you run out of menus in the first six months you are open. We always use 1000 as the magic number when printing for the first time. You should get printing prices on 1000, 2000, 3000, and 5000 pieces. The per-piece cost goes down substantiality with higher quantities. Keep in mind that if you order a large amount, you may be stuck with leftover menus. Every client should be given a menu, especially those that are new. You should also give a salon menu with referral cards. That way, when your loyal clients refer someone to you, they can also give the referred client your salon menu. For your first menu print, we suggest going with a lower quantity so you can make any necessary adjustments and not have waste. But, if you have plans to use the menus for marketing, you may want more. Then, you'll have plenty for bridal show exhibits or Chamber of Commerce events or to leave at retirement community centers, community education centers, college campuses, or local business affiliates.

Special colors or foil on your menu will quickly cause the price of printing to rise. These may be something you can't avoid if you want to show quality and detail. It may be worth the additional investment to have the look and image you are trying to create for your salon.

The cost of each menu will vary depending on paper grade, complex logos, foils, and/or multiple colors. Any of these will increase your printing costs. Depending on your budget, you can spend as little as fifty cents to $2 per menu. You may get away with a much cheaper price depending on the quality and the look you want to achieve. Price the final menu proof with at least three reputable companies. Remember, you get what you pay for in quality and turnaround time.

> **NOTE**
>
> As technology has advanced, we feel that an investment in a high-quality desktop printer will give you great flexibility to change your menu, and in the long term will save you money.

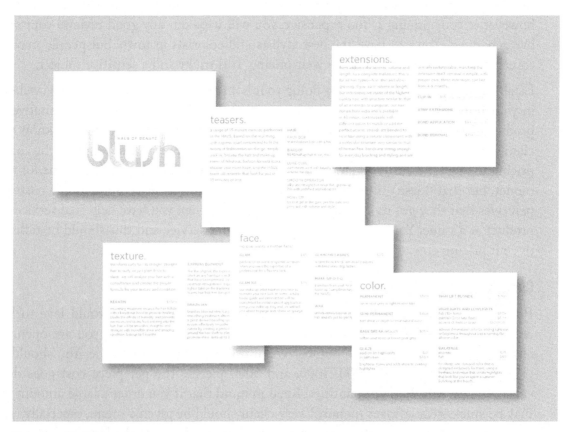

Pages from Blush rate card

CHAPTER 27

Web Presence & Social Marketing

In the world today, every business needs a website. Understanding how your website and social marketing can help your business is critical to your marketing strategy. The first thing that needs to be done when you are getting ready to start your company is to create your salon name and at the same time secure a domain name or your website URL. Before you formalize your legal name, go to companies like Godaddy.com to see if the domain name is available. It is very important in the "big picture" and the amount of exposure that you will receive with the Internet.

Once you've secured the domain name, you can easily set up a basic Web page for free. There are free templates on the Internet that will walk you through a step-by-step process and give you a basic website within a couple of hours, even though you may not be Internet-savvy. Here are some free website tools that you can use to get started:

www.wix.com

www.intuit.com

www.freewebsitetemplates.com

www.sites.google.com

It's also a good idea to think about how people will access your website. If most of your clients are using smart phones, then you need to know that Flash-based sites will not be viewable for those using iPhones. Android or Flash-compatible smartphones will have no problem and are Flash compatible.

The most important thing that you should do when you build your website is to promote a sign-in area and collect email addresses. The information will be critical down the road as far as doing "e-blasts" to your database, running specials of the week, or holding a "blowing out" sale for products that are not moving off the shelves.

Eventually, once your business is up and running and you have your salon software program, you can upgrade your website and make it interactive to your salon software program. Clients can book appointments online, interact with you, and give you good feedback on improving your business. Your website should also have an area for haircuts and color work that you update weekly to develop a portfolio to highlight the styles and the talented stylists at your salon. You can look at using Flickr to share photos.

Your website should also contain a calendar of events, a charity that you support, and "promo" of the week. The offering should be an incredible deal. You want to give reasons for your clients to go on your site every week to see what is coming up next. Your site can really be a vehicle for bringing in business, but it is important that you update and change your site continuously. We recommend you review your site every day and answer feedback quickly. It will help build your business and develop a loyal client base.

> **NOTE**
>
> It's also a good idea to mention clients' special events or charity functions on your website.

One of the biggest concerns or questions that salon owners have about their website is, "How quick can I get on the front/top page of Google or Yahoo, so I can be seen?"

When searching, usually people only scroll through the first two pages of suggested links. Then, they pick from the options or they give up. So, being at or near the top of a search is important. In most cases, a company's search position is an important factor. However, for most salons, being in the forefront of a search engine optimization (SEO) is not critical, unless you are a chain or a school organization. Your website is for your clientele and more for the local market; they will find you by local advertising, personal promoting, and word of mouth. That being said, you should focus some energy on local SEO tactics and list your salon in as many online directories as possible, including Google and Yahoo map directories. This will have the biggest payoff for you from a search standpoint.

If you feel it is important to be on the top of the SEO, then there are two types of websites to discuss.

First, you have the traditional website. What we mean by "traditional" is that it sits there until someone clicks on the site. The way to climb up the ladder is by paying Google to be on the very top for every click that you receive. They may charge you $1.00 per click and if you have 10,000 clicks that month, you need to pay Google $10,000. For a single salon, this is not a cost-effective approach.

Just recently, we were introduced to another way to make a website. It looks like a regular website, but it is designed with WordPress, which is a site that provides you with a method to create a newsletter or blog.

With WordPress, your website is fluid, always changing, and has constant activity. We recommend that before you hire a Web designer, interview several, and see what they have to say before choosing one. The industry is coming up with so many new ideas and concepts for Internet exposure that it is important to listen to several experts in the field to evaluate who you feel can do the best job for you. But, do your research and make sure you check on Search

Engine Optimization myths or scams. Going with a company that is using poor tactics to improve your page rank can actually hurt you in the end.

With your website up and running, what are some other methods to get exposure through the Internet for your salon? Believe it or not, Facebook is a terrific vehicle for getting exposure. We have witnessed several of our friends explode from being known at the local level, to getting noticed nationally, and moving to international success, all from Facebook.

A lot of people use Facebook for personal reasons, but using it for business is extremely successful. You just need to give good content and you will develop a following where people will look for your "tip of the day" or your latest hairstyle for the week. Shooting video of one minute or less and putting that on Facebook is also more effective than pictures. We recommend you establish a YouTube channel account and create a video library. On Facebook, you can create a business page for your salon or a public figure page for yourself. These are all great vehicles for getting exposure and creating a "superstar" image.

Once you become a "superstar" or have people who want to hear what you have to say, Twitter is a great vehicle to go "viral." It is an instant way to have people hear about what is on your mind at any given moment. Maybe you just finished a hair color with a new product. You can describe how it turned out and give your input on the product. You may have just finished a workshop or presentation and you describe the atmosphere and how it feels. With Twitter, you write quick messages to your followers containing 140 characters or less on anything they like. If you have a large following, you can give a tip of the day or send out a tiny "URL," which contains an interesting article, video, etc. With a tiny URL, you can track engagement to find out what people like to hear about and what interests them.

Two other vehicles to increase awareness about you and your business is "blogging," or creating newsletters on the Web. Every time you post something on the Internet, it goes into the "Internet universe" and gets catalogued for future use. By blogging and regularly posting content, you will increase your odds of being found. Plus, you'll become a sought after resource for the salon industry and you'll become more visible to hair salon academies and schools. Be sure to write about the products you carry. For example, salons that carry L'Oreal should write about L'Oreal hair color, L'Oreal product reviews, and recreating looks with L'Oreal products. If someone does a search in Google on "L'Oreal," your articles may come up. It's that simple! So, start writing!

All of the vehicles mentioned above are about making people aware of your work and your business; and it can turn your salon into a profitable entity.

Let's look at some of the statistics on social media:

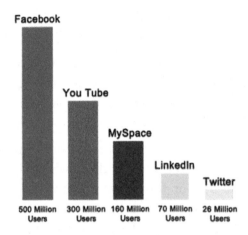

Which One to Use?

The chart below illustrates demographics on who uses each one of these social media avenues.

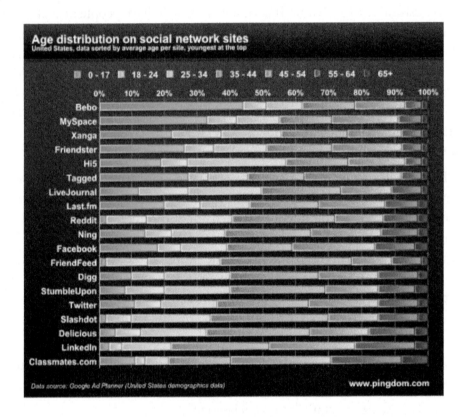

The most surprising factor—the biggest age group for Facebook (with 500 million viewers) is 45 to 54 years old. The average time people spend on Facebook every day is 40 minutes. The usual website time is 1 to 3 minutes.

Facebook

- You can use it for personal or business purposes
- You can import your contact list to search for current Facebook friends
- Personal page
- Up to 5000 friends
- Privacy controls
- Share photos and video
- Can group your friends into lists
- Minimal customization; however, custom tabs and applications can allow for a more personalized look of your page to reflect your personal brand.

Business Page on Facebook

- No limit on number of fans
- Fans don't have to join to see information
- Can control fan interaction (wall posts, etc.)
- Share photos and video
- Bulk messages to fans goes to "updates" and not "inbox messages"
- Statistics on demographics of fans and interactions
- Can personalize applications (e-commerce, custom tabs, etc.)
- Administrators are private, meaning you can hire outside help to keep your page up and running or share the administration with a couple of people

YouTube

- Video sharing
- Can make videos public, unlisted, or private
- Can make videos available to specific users
- Provides embedded HTML codes for adding videos onto any website
- You can create an automatic feed of newly uploaded videos into your website
- You can customize your YouTube channel page to your salon's brand

LinkedIn

- Used primarily for business purposes
- More professional users
- Resembles an online resume
- You can import your contacts and search for current LinkedIn users
- You can integrate your Twitter updates to post automatically to your LinkedIn update
- You can search by individual's name, company, title, location etc.

- "Answers" application allows you to position yourself as an expert
- "Polls" application allows you to create polls and share them on and off of LinkedIn
- You can join groups to ask and answer questions

Twitter

- Referred to as a "micro-blogging" website
- Users are limited to 140 characters in their updates
- Personalization of Twitter page for branding
- Can group the people you follow into lists
- Can "direct message" (private message) individuals
- Mostly used to quickly update followers or send links to relevant information or external sites
- By adding a # before a word, you make it searchable within Twitter (keywords)
- Can reply to someone publicly, for example: @sourcesalonspa
- Courtesy is to "retweet" information others post and to follow back those who follow you

Here are some other tools to consider:
- Ping.FM: automates posts across multiple social media channels
- Tweetdeck: updates Facebook and Twitter simultaneously
- Twitterfeed: feed your blog into Twitter and Facebook
- Hootsuite: allows you to schedule posts across multiple social media channels

Here are our best recommended practices for these social networks:
- Combine your social media efforts with your website
- Repurpose your blog into your social media
- Drive traffic to your website via social media and capture user details
- Include social media icons (links) on your website to your social media pages

Blogs

- Blogs are like an online diary, only in this case don't talk about recent breakups or other personal information, talk about your industry and build your credibility
- They are used to share information in a less formal way
- You can blog about inspiration, business, family, causes, or just about anything you wish
- You can tie in your blog to your website

- They continue to grow in popularity

- Great for SEO (Search Engine Optimization)

- Aside from our home page, we notice that our blog is the second most-visited page on our website

Salon Owner/Operators Discuss the Good, the Bad, & the Ugly

James Jordan

"Went online crazy putting up profiles everywhere I could. Yelp, local Yahoo, blog post, Facebook, MySpace, Yellow Pages online (yellowpages.com), Salon Galaxy, Redken.com, Squidoo, building a website on Yahoo.com, learning about backlinks, SEO (Search Engine Optimization), etc. All these things brought in tons of new clients searching on the Internet for a new stylist."

Diane M. Fedrizzi

"Having a new website for clients to view, to make their appointments by email and $10.00 off coupon for all new clients to print out and bring with them to the salon."

Internet Home Page

CHAPTER 28

Effective Salon Promotions & Loyalty Programs

Marketing is the key to any successful business. Without a serious marketing program for your salon, it will be difficult to attract new clients and keep current clients satisfied. In the current small business climate, you must always think outside the box and stay ahead of your competitors by creating a marketing "buzz." A marketing buzz must be directed at different types of people—current, prospective, and new clients.

Promotional specials can be the key to long-term sustainability in your salon business. Experienced and successful salon owners have been using salon promotions and loyalty programs for years to keep salon traffic flowing, increase sales, and attract new clientele.

The objective of any promotion and loyalty program is to:

- Keep your salon on the minds of your clients

- Get them to book more visits

- Reward them for spending more on services and products in the salon

- Make sure they have such a wonderful experience that they refer you to friends and family

The main goal of these special promotions is to improve client retention through repeat and increased business and growth by referrals. These special offerings should be simple, easy to understand, and not a financial burden to the salon and staff.

Getting Started

The key to a successful promotion should always start with current clients. Dedicating your energy to your best customers is smart business. **Twenty percent of your customers will end up providing 80 percent of your business.** These promotions should always take into consideration what services and products your top clients use when visiting your salon.

Create a Loyalty Path

Customers take loyalty programs very seriously. These programs should make them feel special by you rewarding them for their loyalty and spending their time and money in your salon. When developing these programs, you should always keep in mind that whatever you offer should help them feel important to your business and as though the promotions you offer are geared specifically toward them.

Loyalty Programs Are Long-Term Projects

Loyalty programs have to put be in place for the long-term. You must have the system in place to monitor and keep track of your customers. The worst thing you can do is put a program in place and not give your clients the ability to redeem the promotion you offered.

We recommend having a time frame or expiration date for whatever offering you provide. Doing so will enable you to monitor the promotion. It will also give you the benefit of changing it for the next time or never offering it again. Open-ended promotions are very dangerous and could be extremely expensive.

Action Promotions

The best promotion you can offer in the salon is one that creates such a buzz that it prompts the client to do something the minute they walk in the salon. We call these "action promotions."

> **NOTE**
>
> A good action promotion makes the client feel like they are missing something if they don't take advantage of the special offering right away.

Don't Spend a Lot of Money

The best promotions do not have to cost you a ton of money. A simple promotion can start with your staff. While clients are having services done, let them know what promotions are offering in the salon. The offer of the promotion can start with the receptionist, shampoo assistant, or anyone else who touches your client in the salon. Creating a salon buzz about upcoming promotions is a very inexpensive way to roll out an exciting offering.

Product Promotions

You may find that your manufacturer is offering a promotion. Taking advantage of it could be a very cost-effective way to roll out the same promotion in your salon. You should be able to arrange free samples and advertisements (signs, flyers, promotional samples) from the manufacturer for a special event in your salon.

Create Promotional Collateral

Running a promotion should be fun and engaging for your salon, clients, and staff. Creating flyers, signage, and posts on your website, blog, and social channels should all be part of the promotion. A comprehensive effort will create a message to everyone that you are serious about your promotion and your business.

Promotions That Work

Salons have tried many different programs over the years. What works in one area of the country may not work in another. Demographics play an important role in what you promote in your salon. A salon in a college town may need to offer inexpensive haircuts for students. A small town may not warrant expensive color promotions. A salon in a metropolitan area may need to offer a quicker haircut promotion for the business person who is on the go. We have explored many different promotions from across the country. Here are some ideas that you may use to help grow your business through a successful promotional campaign.

Ten Ideas That Work

1. **Referral Card:** "Refer a friend promotion" is when the existing client and the new client get something for acting on the referral. The existing client gets 20 percent off the total price of services on their next visit. The new client gets $20 off the first $50 they spend or a free bottle of shampoo or conditioner. The dollar amounts and offerings can change. You set the guidelines. Referrals are a great way to get new business and help your staff members to grow their clientele.

2. **25% Off First-Timers:** It's not easy to take away clients from a good competitor, but in these tough times, discounting may be just enough to get them to give your salon a try. You have nothing to lose and everything to gain.

3. **Buy One, Get One Free:** Speak to your product supplier to see if they can help you with a "buy one, get one free" promotion. They may look to move a particular product. It's a no-brainer when it comes to giving something away. It should help you move some overstocked items or get some people window shopping to come into your salon to buy some product. Once they step inside your salon, it's up to you to introduce them to your services by giving them a salon tour and making sure that they get a salon menu.

4. **$10 Off Your Next Service Cards:** Save these cards for the special client or a new client. Give out the card on their birthday, for a special event, or to brighten up their day. Ten dollars may not seem like a lot, but it will make them feel special and remember your salon and staff.

5. **10% Off Pre-Booking Discount:** It's great when your client leaves your salon with a smile and loves the way she looks, but sometimes it is not enough to ensure that they will come back. Make sure they return by giving them 10 percent off by pre-booking their next appointment.

6. **$25 Off on Your Birthday:** Birthdays are a special event, but sometimes overlooked. Why not give your client a birthday to remember? Offer a discount of $25—that will surely put a smile on their face. They will be on the phone or texting their friends about how nice your salon and staff treated them or remembered them on their birthday.

7. **Girls' Night Out:** Pick your slowest night at the salon and offer free services or product promotions. Give out invitations to your clients and tell them they can bring as many people as they want. Have some wine and cheese and make some nice product packages that are not too expensive, all for about $20 and under. People will feel obligated to make a purchase. What a great way to increase business on a slow night! Offer a special discount to those who book an appointment that night.

8. **20% Off Any Additional Services:** When a client is sitting in your chair and they say they have time to kill, offer 20 percent off any additional services that they normally would not have booked. They will be happy with the additional service and feel good about the discount on something they may not have thought about having done.

9. **Local Business Gathering:** Use your salon as a meeting place for professionals or other businesses in your area. Have a once-a-month social gathering to meet the business owners next door or around the corner. What a great way for you and your staff to meet potential new clients and help spread the word about your salon. Don't let them leave empty-handed. Always give an inexpensive gift or product with your name and number or at least your business card or a first-time discount coupon.

10. **Free Haircut or Color With Fifth Visit:** You must have a system to keep track of this, but what a nice thing to keep your clients loyal. You can also allow them to bank the free haircut and use it for product or a more expensive service as they continue to visit the salon.

Salon Owner/Operators
Discuss the Good,
the Bad, & the Ugly

Glenn Guerriero

"We create news and the media reports it. We also do a lot of free stuff. And remember, pictures, pictures, pictures at shows and more pictures, because you have to be seen to be known. All this and develop an informative website on who you are and what makes you different. Then find all the websites where you can list your salon for free. Be different and trust your skills; don't be afraid of changing."

Nina Dalaco, Eastin Myles

"Be more than the clients expect. Surprise them with a complementary value-added service. Have a special VIP client of the day and take lots of pictures. CELEBRATE—anything. It adds interest and excitement. Post awards of things your staff does RIGHT. The clients love to see that. Keep a promotional calendar, every 8 weeks. That will allow a special to be available at each client visit rotation. Do a fund-raiser for your community; it creates good will. Have a special wine and cheese party for VIP clients and have your distributor do a client-focused presentation and give samples. The opportunities are endless."

Christopher Theman, Behind the Chair

"You have to give to get. My program for the last 30 years has been to have all my hairdressers do a free haircut, then 50% off the second cut, then full price on the third cut. If they don't own them by the last cut, they're doing something wrong. We need to talk!"

Tammy Boykins

"Marketing to brides and participating in bridal shows and events. We also take advantage of different seasonal services and events."

CHAPTER 29

Your Mission Statement

"Leadership is based on spiritual quality; the power to inspire, the power to inspire others to follow."

—Vince Lombardi

What is a mission statement? Why do you need one? How does it help? What is the purpose?

A mission statement tells something about who you are, what your salon represents, and your reason for being in business.

A mission statement is a short, written statement of the purpose of a company or organization. The mission statement should guide the actions of the organization, spell out its overall goal, and guide decision making.

For example, our mission statement for this book is, "To help aspiring salon owners develop and achieve their dream of owning a successful salon." With that said, we have written this book with the purpose of giving the first-time entrepreneur a better chance of being a success. We hope that, after you read this, you will have a better understanding of what it takes to create your dream.

Writing a mission statement should not be difficult. You need to ask yourself some key questions about why you went into business, what business are you in, and who you are in business for. In your case, it is owning a salon. You want to define an effective way to get your message out.

The message has to convey "the why and the wow" behind your company. It is not only for your clients, but your employees as well.

Here are a few suggested tips to assist you with writing your mission statement:

- Clearly state your goals and objectives.
- Decide what makes you different. Do you offer greater value? Are you better or faster than the salon nearby?

- Build your brand.
- Keep it short and sweet.
- Be honest.
- Make it "sizzle."
- State the facts and why.

We recommend that you create yours at the very beginning of your business venture. Following are some examples of mission statements:

- Making a difference with every cut
- Creating a new look for every client
- Making a difference in the world
- Making your dream cut a reality
- Creating a better world with a better look
- Caring for life's journeys
- One person, one change, one vision
- Making a difference and giving back to each client
- Sharing our expertise with the world
- Pay it forward one cut at a time
- Cutting a path to give back
- Giving joy to all clients
- Committed to making a better planet
- Committed to fulfilling dreams for each client
- Giving back to the world by cutting perfection for every client
- Giving smiles to each client, one cut at a time

You should find yourself—and your employees—referring to the mission statement regularly. You must look for ways to connect your mission statement with the tasks you do every day. Clients ought to understand and agree with your mission statement.

Don't just write one to check it off the list, file it away, and forget about it. This gives the impression that the mission statement is unnecessary. Use these guidelines to create your own mission statement. Make it part of your salon menu and communicate your mission with employees when you bring them onboard.

As your business grows and you hone in on your competitive advantage, look at your mission statement and change it up. You may find that your business focuses on a particular segment of the market or that you and your staff excel at a particular set of services. Involve your staff, discuss your mission, and write it together. It should feel right.

CHAPTER 30

Developing the Salon Culture

"Loose tongues are worse than wicked hands."

—Jewish Proverb

Capturing Your Codes of Conduct & Ethics

Putting your codes of conduct and rules in place will not happen overnight. To determine your codes, go out and visit with other salons as a customer. Break down how you were treated in each environment. Try different services in each salon you visit. Purchase retail in each salon. Pay attention to how the staff dressed and treated you. Were they kind and courteous? Did they ask you if you would like a cup of coffee? Did they give you a salon tour?

Pretend you are a secret shopper, make notes of your experience, and put it in a file. Each salon will be different. Think about what you would do differently and what codes of conduct would need to be in place to create the experience that you want at your salon.

Capturing your codes is not just based on other businesses. Following your instincts and how you like to be treated as a person will also be a big factor in your approach. Your staff and customers will respect a work environment built on a strong code of conduct with business, security, sensitivity, and compassion as its foundation.

You already know how you service clients and what works best for you. It's time to start thinking about how you will teach others and hold your staff accountable on how you want your clients treated.

Ethics

What are the benefits of having a set code of ethics at your salon? Ethical standards will protect your salon's clients as well as the stylists and the salon owner(s).

A business code of ethics is a set of rules and principles that defines how you want your salon to be run, how employees should dress, how to treat clients, how to sell to clients, and how the salon will operate day-to-day. A set code of ethics establishes rules, communicates expectations, and sets the bar straight for simple things where black and white moral judgments may not apply. Your clients will always feel they are in a professional atmosphere and continue to come back and recommend your salon to others.

By putting the business code of ethics into an employee handbook, you will set the foundation for your salon's culture from the moment you start your business. Waiting to set these guidelines is a mistake; you should define them before you interview or hire your first employee. Explain your business code of ethics to job candidates and reinforce the codes once you hire the employee and begin the training process. Salons with a strong code of ethics that are followed daily will have satisfied customers and a happy staff because everyone will know what is expected.

Respect & Integrity

A code of ethics promotes an environment of respect and integrity. When your staff knows your code and follows it, this creates an atmosphere of trust, respect, and confidence in the actions of each person involved in your salon. When you have a written code of ethics, your employees are expected to behave a certain way toward each other and your clients. The result of this is a more peaceful atmosphere where employees can focus on serving the clients without the problems that come about from mixing many different personalities into one "small" space. A code of ethics is only effective if your staff believes and knows that your rules will be enforced.

Trust & Honesty

A code of ethics is your salon's rule book. Rules promote trust and honesty, especially when practiced on a daily basis. When one of your employees breaks one of the codes of ethics, the problem should be dealt with immediately. Don't wait.

All of your employees should learn from their mistakes. Don't dwell on it. Address it, allow improvement for the violation, and move on. Always conduct yourself in an ethical manner. Your rule book should have one very important code—treat others as you would like to be treated yourself.

NOTE
Discuss with your staff that gossiping is a breakdown of your code of ethics.

Confidentiality is very important. A client who has a problem and confides in your staff should not have to worry about hearing what they said from a stranger.

Responsibility Is Your Duty

Be responsible. This is the most important rule to follow as an owner, manager, and/or employee. When people take responsibility for their actions, everyone benefits. Responsibility is accountability and honesty, and holding yourself accountable promotes good character traits in others who see them in you. It helps to create a cohesive and productive work environment which will enable you to have longer employee retention. Employees are more likely to continue working for a company that follows and promotes rules that protect and benefit everyone's equality.

Salon Owner/Operators Discuss the Good, the Bad, & the Ugly

Annamaries Lignori, Beautiful Cuts Hair Salon

"I set my intentions with my staff daily. We all follow the simple rules I put in place. They all have respect for each other. The most important rule we follow is, 'The customer is always right no matter what.'"

Doreen C, Grooming Styling Salon

"I have a sign that hangs in the dispensary that only my staff can see. They have to read it daily. It reads, 'Be empowered to create a unique, memorable, and personal experience for your clients! Love what you do and love the people you work with!'"

Rosalind Anderson-Holsey

"My biggest mistake was thinking everyone would embrace the vision for the salon and trusting staff to carry out the same goals when I wasn't there. A boat has the potential to sink without the captain guiding it. One small hole will still allow water in the boat. Stay on deck and let passion be the energy you need to move your business!"

Lee Ann Hopkins

"Not paying more attention to what my partner was doing, or not doing. Too much trust."

Rose Rodgers-Stauffer

"Not creating a culture of developing others to do the work the way I do!"

CHAPTER 31

Tipping

"You have to tip your stylist "big time." Those magic fingers keep
you looking young, hot, and sexy. One bad haircut and color can
run you out of town!"

—Unknown actress

Tipping is always optional. Grooming industry workers have grown accustomed to tips being part of their income. If you combine other services with a haircut, the tip amount can be very large. However, if your customer is not happy in a particular circumstance, they may not provide a tip.

In this chapter, we will educate you as the salon owner/barber/stylist on what is expected of you with your clients and how much of a tip to expect for the services you offer your customer. The grooming industry is a service industry that is widely known to be a tipped service. Normally, the guide used is 15 percent of the pre-tax bill. Most people tip on the entire amount of the bill for the sake of simplicity or to be a bit more generous.

Tips From the Employer's Perspective

Many salon owners determine salaries on the skills that a new hire may have. Experience, the level of the position, the salary ranges within the geographic area of the salon, and the current economic conditions in the market all impact the decision.

The salon owner has the ability to use tipping in their favor as a tool to hire more talented and experienced hair stylists. The fact that a salon may be located in a very high-end area or charge more for their services due to their reputation means that most employees in that salon will earn more in salary and tips. It's very simple—the higher the price for the service and the better the quality of the service being offered equals much higher tips. In fact, salon owners and stylists or other service providers have greater earning potential. This is a win-win for all.

The Who, What, & Why of Tipping

Salon Coupons or Gift Certificates: If your customer received a coupon or gift certificate to your salon for a specific dollar amount, then that dollar amount should be treated the same as cash. The customer should be able to tip with the card. To keep things easier, you may offer to have the customer tip with cash and not use the card. The tip should always be based on the price of the service regardless of the value of the gift card.

Expensive Service: If your hair salon is in a high-end area and your services are expensive, that doesn't mean your customers should tip less because of the prices you charge. High-priced services, such as a haircut and color, hair extensions, or a hair straightening, warrant a larger tip. If the service being offered is done with the best of care and quality, you and your staff should be tipped accordingly.

Tipping the Owner: This is one of the most controversial areas for clients and owners. Years ago it was not common practice to tip the owner. If you own the salon and you are providing the service, then you should be tipped. It is up to you, as the owner, to take the tip or not. So, the question is, "Do they or don't they tip you as the owner of the salon or barber shop?" The answer to this question is, "Yes, your clients should still tip you!"

Tipping for the Holidays: The holidays are a great time of year for salon services because everyone wants to look great at their holiday parties. We, as service providers, look forward to an extra-large tip from our clients, but should it be expected? Do your clients have to provide you with an extra holiday tip bonus? It is normal for your clients to tip you if you have provided them with a service all year long. The order of tipping should start with your shampoo person. He or she should expect $10, stylists an extra $20, and a manicurist, $15. Remember, tipping is discretionary; make sure your staff knows this and they should not expect to base their salary and their lifestyle on customers' tips.

How Tips Are Collected

Tips are normally collected when paying for your service. We have seen many different variations that have worked in salons, barbershops, and/or spas. As the salon owner, it is up to you to decide how you want tips to be collected and given back to the person who performed the service.

What works the best and gives a professional touch to your place of business is the envelope system. You should have envelopes for each of your service providers. These envelopes should have their name, the date, and the services offered. When your customer is finished paying, they can place the tip in the envelope. This takes away the embarrassment of handling money and deciding on where to place the tip and who to give it to. The client can hand the envelope over to the service provider or back to the checkout person. It's nice, neat, and clean. It also provides a solution to a client who is wondering if they should tip or not. If you hand the client an envelope, then it is suggesting that your salon and service provider is expecting a tip. If the client is confused, your front desk person should be ready to assist.

Does your salon:

○ Educate employees about reporting tips to the IRS and state agencies, if applicable?

○ Have established tip reporting procedures?

○ Give out reports on payday about how much in tips the employees have received during that pay period?

○ Stay current with all employer tax payments and filing obligations?

○ Give out Form 4070 from the IRS for employees to report tips earned?

○ Encourage employees to report tips earned?

○ Explain in detail that unreported tips can result in a tax obligation to the IRS with penalties at the end of the year?

Suggested Tip Ranges

- Hairdresser/stylist: 15 percent or more, $3 to $5 dollars extra for last minute service, such as an eyebrow waxing or a nail touch-up.

- Salon or spa package: If your salon or spa does not charge a service fee, then your service providers should expect to split a 15 to 20 percent tip. You should leave envelopes at the front desk.

- Manicurist/pedicurist: 10 to 15 percent of total service.

- Hair assistant: $5 to $10 handed directly to the person.

- Massage therapist: 10 to 15 percent.

- Electrolysis/hair removal: 10 percent.

- Hair extensions: 10 to 20 percent regardless of the cost of service.

- Shoe shine: $2 per pair of shoes.

- Barber: 10 to 15 percent on the total service.

- Hair extensions: 10 to 20 percent.

- Shampoo person: $2 to $5 handed directly to the shampoo person.

- Front desk: Typically, there is no tip for the front desk, but if they help with an early check-in or late checkout or a retail purchase, then the tip is usually $1 to $2.

- Coat check person: $1 dollar.

- Major makeover or color correction: If you did something out of the ordinary for your client, you should expect a higher tip than normal. That may exceed 20 percent.

Remember that tipping is discretionary. If your client doesn't think they have to tip your shampoo girl, they may not. If they feel that the service they received was not as expected, they may not tip you and your staff the expected amount or anything at all. It is not a moral obligation to tip. That said, if you are relying on tips for paying your bills in the salon or at home, you may want to rethink this business model. Tips are normally a gracious way to say thank you for the service received. Make sure that every time you pick up your scissors or clippers you are trying your best to create a masterpiece. This will be reflected in your overall tip.

The tipping guidelines are for services being rendered in a salon, as a booth renter, or if working out of the house. Again, these are customary tips, but your clients may not be educated on proper tipping for services. Although you expect a tip for your services, you cannot count on them as a regular part of your salary.

> **Salon Owner/Operators Discuss the Good, the Bad, & the Ugly**

Santina's Barber Shop, Los Angeles

"Any which way you slice it, you have to report your tips. Therefore, I report them on Form 4070 at the end of each pay period. In my case, that's twice a month."

JT's Brazen Cutz Barber Shop, Wilmington, NC

"Tips are never a guarantee. To me, they are an incentive to do a great job. If I don't, my tips are affected. I always tell my staff, 'Your tips have to be earned. When your pockets are empty, it's time to do better, quality work.'"

CHAPTER 32

Customers Have Feelings Too

"We are ladies and gentlemen serving ladies and gentlemen."
—The Ritz Carlton motto

You can do everything imaginable to create a top-notch salon, but this will not guarantee that your clients are happy and that you will make them feel important. Many of us forget to think about our clients and their feelings when we are so wrapped up in our own.

All of us want to feel as though we matter. Think about the last time someone went out of their way to make you feel special. I bet you can clearly remember what you felt like, what you needed, and how that person made your day by doing something special for you. The point is, we remember when someone goes out of their way to make us feel special. It can be a very small gesture, but it creates a bond between the giver and the receiver. It doesn't even have to be a material thing; but, whatever it is, we are sure to remember it and talk about it. It makes us go out of our way to be around that person or their place of business. People gravitate to those who make them feel special.

What can your salon do that will not cost you anything, but create warm feelings about your salon? The actions must start at your front desk and follow throughout the entire salon.

Use Your Clients' Names

The easiest thing to do is to use your client's name. Your front desk professional knows the client is coming in at a certain time. The appointment is on her computer or logged in in the appointment book. How nice to be greeted with, "Good morning, Mrs. Client! It's so nice to see you again. We are looking forward to taking care of you today."

Wow. Was that hard? No, of course not, but that's the first step. The second step is when the shampoo person greets the same customer and uses his or her name again. These are examples of easy ways to make someone feel extremely special. Do you do this in your salon today? You have their names, use them.

Acknowledge Them

We all have experienced waiting in line for something. Most of the time, we have gone out of our way to be at a specific place at a specific time. Has anyone ever said they are sorry for making you wait? When you go unnoticed, you feel that your time is not valued.

Well, your client's time is valuable too. They have families like you and they have put forth some effort to make it on time to their appointment with you.

When your client is sitting there in the waiting area, acknowledge them. Walk over and smile and say hello. Shake their hand; give them a hug. These small things minimize the fact that you may be running late. Remember a time when you were ignored—you don't want your client to experience that and develop bad feelings about you or your salon.

Apologize

Don't think your salon and staff will never run into problems. With so many variables, it seems that something could go wrong at any time—personality clashes, chemicals being mixed incorrectly or spilled, misbehaving or dull scissors, electrical equipment failure, and plumbing or hot water issues. In fact, you might think, "How is it that more bad things don't happen in a given day?" Whatever the circumstance, the client is always right. When things do go wrong, make sure you and your staff simply say, "We are sorry." An apology goes a long way. It is a simple way to build a loyal client. The better person always apologizes first; don't let your ego get in the way. You may also have to be prepared to give a full refund or cover the service for the day at no charge to the client. This will depend on the mishap that occurred, but you should be ready for this or other recovery gifts in the event that something goes wrong.

Listen

How many times has someone said to you, "Are you listening to me?" Maybe it's your children, spouse, or clients. Most people can tell when you are listening to them and when your mind is somewhere else. It makes people feel important when you give them 100 percent of your attention and really listen to what they are saying. Your customer may be going through an illness, a divorce, or work-related problems. Listening to their stories is important to them because true listening in today's world is rare. Sometimes you might feel more like a counselor than a hairstylist. If you are developing a close bond with your client, they will share their good and bad news. A shoulder to cry on is part of the job and part of the service you provide. If you have to apply a hair color or give a haircut, why not pay attention to your client at the same time? If it makes them feel good, go out of your way to be a good listener.

Training your salon team to become good listeners is very important. They are representing your company. You want to make sure they are applying the exact color or giving the hairstyle your client asks for. It's not always the story you have to listen to, but the service your client is asking for.

Make Them Part of Something

It is crucial to make your client feel a part of your business. Sometimes, it means you have to think out of the box to include them. If your distributor is offering education to your staff, include some of your clients. Have them come in for a free service and use them as models. Involving them will bring them closer to you and your staff.

If you are having a "Ladies Night Out," include some clients to make them feel special. They may not participate, but the invitation will surely let them know that they were considered. Sometimes, the thought is all that matters in making someone's day.

Thank You

The easiest way to make any client feel good and appreciated is to say, "Thank you!" It doesn't cost you a thing to show how much you appreciate the fact that you have loyal customers who keep coming back to your salon. How many times have you forgotten to say thank you?

We stated in the beginning of this chapter that saying hello and using the client's name is important. It is just as important to say goodbye and thank you, using their name as you close out their service and visit for the day.

The following has worked for over 25 years, "Thank you for your business. As always, it is a pleasure having you at my salon. Your continued business is appreciated by me and my family as well."

All of us should implement these practices at work each day. When we do, it will make our work more enjoyable and create a strong legion of clients who will continue to support our business.

CHAPTER 33

How to Hire Quality Service Providers for Your Salon

Written by Jill Krahn, Senior Vice President of Sales, The Salon Professional Academies Franchise Group.

""Teamwork is the ability to work together toward a common vision, the ability to direct individual accomplishments toward organizational objectives. It is the fuel that allows common people to attain uncommon results."

—Andrew Carnegie

The first step in hiring quality service providers for your salon is building a relationship with cosmetology schools who maintain high standards and graduation rates. It is important to build a rapport with area cosmetology establishments in order to stay informed about current events involving both students and staff, such as career and demonstration days. These events allow students and staff of the cosmetology establishment to become familiar with your salon, while also allowing management to see the personalities of students in their learning environment. It is vital to become involved in advisory boards at cosmetology schools, which provide opportunities for salon owners to give feedback to the cosmetology establishment regarding what they would like to see in new hires.

Selectively choosing service providers ensures a standard of quality performance; thereby building on the reputation and success of your salon. When preparing yourself to hire service providers, find out if the cosmetology schools you have a relationship with have a placement program. If the students in surrounding establishments do not seem like a good fit for your salon, be prepared to travel to another city in search of a future employee. The retention rate of service providers at your salon can increase by as much as 80 percent if you are willing to invest the time and energy into the hiring process.

During the interview process, it is important to review the applicant's high school and cosmetology school attendance records. Their attendance at school is a possible indication of the employee's future attendance habits at your salon. It is often beneficial to ask the interviewee to describe someone who has been a role model in their life. Their answer will give you possible insight to the character and work ethic of this potential employee. In order to finalize which student is the best fit for your salon, have the student perform a full makeover or work alongside you for a day.

Upon hiring, make it clear that you are hiring him or her on a trial or temporary basis, easing the dismissal of an employee who is not meeting expectations. It is essential that all team members are made aware of current expectations and job descriptions. Meeting with new employees daily instills teamwork and the salon's values and ethics with the employee. Setting aside 15 minutes each day to meet with the team member provides an opportunity to discuss daily goals, enabling the employee to take ownership for his/her daily performance. Implementing a training program to test and guide employees is a fundamental growth-building tool which can assist in long-term employee performance.

Be careful not to micromanage your team, as this may stunt creativity. Employees with an open mind will be more receptive to learning. Employees who engage in effective communication with both clients and team members often create an unforgettable customer service experience. As others will look to you for direction, post a positive thought daily to inspire your team. Remember, unexpected services will bring the most value.

First Impression

Ensure that all your employees know the importance of a first impression. Whether the employee handles the front desk, is a master colorist, hairstylist, manicurist, manager, or assistant, everyone contributes to the tone for the entire visit. It is important that everyone looks their best, follows the salon's dress code, and presents themselves with confidence. Make sure you coach your team on smiling, making eye contact, and greeting each other and your clients with a friendly "hello" and a handshake. Make sure you teach the new hire to know and understand the client handling cycle and how to properly move them through the cycle to maximize the experience and income for the salon.

Consultation

Stylists should learn about and master the consultation. This is where the true relationship begins between a service provider and the client. They should discuss what the client is looking for, what they like, or what they'd like to change. Staying positive and making informed, knowledgeable suggestions, including an explanation of tools, techniques, and products is what the provider needs to offer to show expertise. Plant the seed for subsequent visits and retail products that will help the client maintain their look at home and make their new style and/or color last longer.

Service

During the service, it's important that providers incorporate education into the conversation about what they are doing, call attention to the name of the specific products, and explain how to use the product. Establish reasonable expectations for what the product can and cannot do to help the client with any beauty challenges. Providers should "wow" each client with the service and experience—that's what keeps them coming back, referring their friends, trying new services, purchasing products, buying gift certificates, and more. Keep the conversation appropriate, make notes about the visit, formulas, and recommendations. Be sure to summarize everything that was covered with the client.

Recap

At the end of the service, providers should take the time to review the ticket, talk about pre-booking so that they can come back, and freshen up their look right on time. They should also grab any recommended products on their way up to the front desk and mention the ones that were used and that the front desk person can help them with any questions about the products. Additionally, you will be in a prime position to ask for referrals at this point—always ask for referrals and provide them with referral cards.

Reconnect

Let your providers know that you expect them to communicate in some fashion with their clients on a regular basis. They can send a note, a text, or make a quick call—whatever is most appropriate for the relationship that they have with that client.

Providers should check in to:

- See how their clients are doing, especially if they got a totally new look.
- Follow up on a special event that the client may have mentioned.
- Simply say "hi" and invite them in again for a new service being offered at the salon or a specially priced service.

Make sure you give a clear explanation of what is important and what is expected when working with a client in your salon.

Example:

Teach new stylists how to communicate or relate to the client—how to engage the client, ask the client questions, and listen to the client. All of these are important communication tactics to teach a new hire so that they will represent your salon well and give the best customer service to your clients.

The next step is to teach them your expectations of professionalism. Examples: Rate them on their appearance, check the language they choose when talking with the client, and listen to the topics that they talk about. Always train them on the products and services so that you can ensure they have the correct knowledge. Every now and then, test your employees. But, don't set them up for failure. Let them know that you will be doing "pop quizzes on Tuesdays" to test everyone's knowledge about a new product line or about the new customer service guidelines that you reviewed at the last staff meeting.

When you catch people in the act of doing exactly as you want and expect, give them an "on-the-spot" reward. It can be as simple as saying, "Mary, I really like how you reviewed all the features and benefits of the new frizz control product line with your client. I think you should jot down what you said so that we can share the script with the other team members. Looks like it worked too. I saw that she bought the shampoo and conditioner before she left today. Great job!" You can also have gift cards to places like local movie theatres, Starbucks, gas cards, etc. Use these as rewards when your employees meet their daily, weekly, or monthly goals.

We also believe that the employee attitude will determine their "altitude" in their career and their financial success. Look for their: demeanor, posture, personality, and confidence. A grading system will help the new employee have clear and concise knowledge of your salon's expectations.

The results will determine the quality of service that this employee will give your clients, and the relationships that they will build for your salon. With this measurement system in place, you will see the new employee give your client a "wow" factor, meaning the client got more in service than they expected. Doing so will ensure that you have a five-star salon and team.

The winning solution is to prepare and keep score of accomplishments and reward great results. A wise man once told me he would walk in the back door of his businesses and talk to everyone on the way up to the front. By the time he made it to the front, he had a good "pulse" on what was happening in his businesses.

Our advice is to get connected right away to a branding and marketing firm to help drive people to your business; and then, you can wow them with customer service from there.

Salon Owner/Operators
Discuss the Good,
the Bad, & the Ugly

Albie Mulcahy

"Expecting too much at the beginning. Having too many hairdressers to start. You have to feed them."

Barri Allen

"Assuming all hairdressers are professional and eager to be successful."

Sharon Wiser

"I am an instructor and the biggest mistake I see is that people panic hire. They hire bodies instead of hiring the right stylist for their salon. To me, it should be very serious, as employees should be the #1 asset. The interviewer does not follow up and they should have the applicant do several interviews and a technical or performance-based interview as well."

Ian Gavet

"Getting the best people around me."

Judy Rice

"If you are going to be a team, you must play like a team. The strong culture this has created is amazing. Love my staff and salon."

Reggie Stephens

"Biggest mistake made when opening the salon? Overpaying everyone we hired. Build your business plan on real numbers, and pay based on what benefits you will offer. Don't overpay to get someone in. Build your reputation on quality and then the right people will want to work for you, versus you wanting them to work for you."

Jon Gonzales

"As a salon owner, I invest in my salon's greatest profit potential—educating my staff on how to reach higher levels of educational excellence. If I can show them how to triple their income, I triple profits. Always deal in terms of their benefits, not yours. As salon owners, we must set our own quality control and educational standards. My motivation to teach is a little different from beauty school. If I don't teach them well, I go out of business."

Stephen Adams

"Keep growing staff. Train, retain guests, and give great service. Also promote a lot through grass roots such as postcards. Small promos to get new guests in the door. Build on return guests ... add on services, and asking for referrals—nothing new. Just trying to be more consistent."

CHAPTER 34

The Importance of a Gatekeeper

How many times have we walked into a place of business and we were not greeted by someone? It may be a clothing store, restaurant, doctor's office, or a beauty salon. How does that make you feel?

We find ourselves wondering if we should leave. Is the place open for business? We don't know if we should sit or stand or yell hello to see if someone is going to help. The importance of a gatekeeper is crucial to your business.

Historically, the gatekeeper has had many job titles, such as receptionist, secretary, or salesperson. You'll read more in the next chapter about giving the person who initiates first contact a more fitting name for their position. Right now, what matters most is that you realize how critical this person is to the success of your business.

This is the first person your clients meet when they walk into your salon. He or she is the first person who speaks on behalf of your company when a potential client calls or an existing one is making an appointment, or a distributor is calling for assistance in placing a product order. In essence, this person speaks for you and is an extension of you and your salon's brand.

When hiring, have you thought about the personality and character of this individual? Are you certain this person is outgoing and enjoys being around people? There are certain things you should look for when hiring this person. Listed below are several key items to keep in mind when you are interviewing for your gatekeeper:

- Basic understanding of the beauty industry and terminology
- Appearance is very important
- Should have basic research skills
- Outgoing, "people person"
- Should understand and be able to use all office equipment

- Handle all phone calls
- Desire to take charge
- Understanding and ability to use salon's software
- Sales background
- Willing to work full-time, including weekends
- Capable of being your right-hand person
- Capable of handling money
- Trustworthy
- Willing to manage

Marketing, advertising, and word of mouth bring valuable people into your business daily. It takes an investment of time, energy, and money to market the salon, build your brand, and secure loyal clients.

Once you have a new client, your team does their very best to give great customer service and cultivate and maintain a relationship. So, why do so many salon owners hire someone without the background and skills to run and manage the front end of their business?

Most of the time, it's about the money and not thinking of the full scope of responsibilities at the front desk. Please keep in mind that you get what you pay for. Yes, this person will increase your overhead, but he or she will be worth it if you find the right person. It will also take time to train this person, but let's look at the upside. Your gatekeeper should grow into your right-hand person; in time, this is what they should be expected to do for you and your business:

- Answer phones
- Develop client relationships
- Answer routine client questions
- Order supplies
- Handle all credit and cash transactions
- Input all new clients into the system
- Manage all calls and book new appointments
- Maintain a salon "To Do List"
- Maintain office supplies and toiletries
- Handle all software updates and changes
- Assist in all product sales
- Educate clients on products
- Keep clients happy while waiting
- Greet clients in a warm and friendly manner
- Thank your clients when they arrive and when they leave

- Allow you to oversee your daily salon business without major interruptions
- Deal with routine matters
- Process mail

As this person grows into his or her position, the hours that you would normally spend doing the above mentioned items should decrease dramatically. The freed-up time should be spent doing things that normally get put on the back burner, such as marketing and educating staff, and giving your clients great service while strengthening your relationship with them. More importantly, this person will enable you to spend more quality time with family and friends.

It's important to have continuous training and employee development. Either send your key people to beauty trade shows or arrange education classes in your salon through your distributor or software company. Management and/or business classes at your local high school or college can assist in developing key people in your salon.

The key thing is, stay focused on your goals—to better serve clients, develop strong relationships with your clients' friends, and establish better quality of life with your family. The right gatekeeper will make this possible.

When hiring your gatekeeper, be sure to ask:

○ What type of computer skills do you have?

○ Have you ever deposited money at a bank?

○ Have you done credit card processing before?

○ Are you able and capable of opening and closing the salon?

○ Can you work weekends?

○ What type of phone skills do you have?

○ Do you understand and follow time management?

○ Can you take a tough phone call?

○ How do you handle people who are rude or upset?

CHAPTER 35

People Skills for Profitability—at Your Front Desk

Written by Kristi Valenzuela, Salon Success Coach, Crystal Focus Salon Coaching

You've probably heard the saying, "Don't sweat the small stuff?" Sometimes, I think we sweat the small stuff because we don't know there is a bigger problem lurking right over our heads! Every day salon owners are frustrated with the cash drawer being off at the end day by $5 to $20. I realize this feels like lost money and can be disappointing, but did you know that you could be missing **thousand of dollars** every month by not having a properly scripted front desk sales team?

The fastest way to turn your "receptionist team" into a team of extremely professional customer service sales professionals is to first recognize where the challenges are. Once you identify the challenges, you can work on them one step at a time to develop systems and solutions for your salon.

TOP TEN CHALLENGES OF ACHIEVING FRONT DESK EXTREME SALES

1. High turnover at the front desk
2. Recruiting challenges in finding and hiring qualified front desk professionals
3. Ineffective front desk training program
4. Team resistance to front desk
5. Lack of front desk goals and sales
6. Absence of reward system
7. Motivating sales follow-through by leader
8. Inconsistency in scripting
9. Daily missed sales opportunities
10. Understanding when to let go (firing someone)

If you are a salon owner who has owned your business for one month or 20 years, you can probably relate to a few of the above challenges. Now, let's look at the **Top Ten Things You Need To Know To Grow Your Front Desk.**

1. Your Front Desk Is a Profit Center

The front desk is often looked at as a focused area of customer service and first impression. While this is true, the front desk is also an area of extreme revenue potential. Five main areas of focus are gift cards, additional services, pre-booking, referrals, and retail sales. As a salon owner, you should be analyzing your numbers in these profit principles on a monthly basis, recording trends that you see from year-to-year, and planning for service and product promotions. Use your front desk as your front line to increase sales by providing scripts and goals for each of these revenue areas.

2. Hire Qualified Sales People

High turnover is often caused by not having the "right person for the right position." Often, salon owners or managers are hiring out of emergency due to an immediate opening at the front desk. To find the right person, get focused, get organized, and get prepared for the recruiting and interview process. First, you should plan on finding and interviewing several candidates, not just one or two.

The best way to recruit for this position is to find someone that already has customer service and sales experience and possesses "sales charisma." Keep your eyes and ears open for your next front desk person through your own customer service experiences. What about the wait person at your favorite restaurant, who offers an appetizer, deliciously describes her favorite menu item, and reminds you to save room for dessert? What about the person working at your favorite retail store who talks about their loyalty program, gift cards, or special sales?

When it's time to interview, tailor the interview questions around the important duties of a front desk sales support staff. Remember, the front desk is the first impression, the last impression, and often the LASTING impression of the salon.

The people who WOW you should work for you. Don't wait until you need someone! Interview often, even if you don't have an opening! This will improve your interview skills, keep qualified people on file, and keep your existing front desk on their toes! Wouldn't you be on your toes if you knew the owner was always looking for someone for your position?

If you put an ad in the paper, on craigslist.com, or other places, be sure to put your ad in the SALES section, not the receptionist section. This is a sales position.

During the interview, make sure to explain all the sales responsibilities the front desk team has, including offering additional services, pre-booking the next appointment, closing the retail sale, taking clients on a solon tour, offering sales and promotions, etc.

One interview exercise we discuss on the Chapter 2 Hiring audio CD in The Front Desk Doctor training series is called, "Sell me this pen." This is the point in an interview when you would hand your ink pen to the person you are interviewing. Using this performance-based interviewing technique will allow you to see how well they can describe the features and benefits of the pen and offer the sale of the pen to you. Plus, you'll be able to test and see how brave their sales skills really are! You will find, or eliminate, many candidates with this simple exercise. Try it!

3. Train Sales Skills

Each front desk professional should be trained on the services you offer. The ultimate way to train your team is to have them experience the service. Create a 60-day service training commitment in your front desk training of a new team member. Make sure the service provider and the front desk team member stay focused on talking about the service. The front desk team member should take notes on what the features and benefits of the services are, as well as key haircare products that are usually recommended after the service. Finally, they should write a script on how they would offer this service to a client. Review these notes with them and role play their script. Keep these in the employee's work file.

4. Salon Tours

Your front desk person should be well-scripted and well-trained in what makes your salon "different" than the competition. Whether your salon is 8000 square feet or 800 square feet, a salon tour is a critical place to start with a new client. Your tour can take a client on a walk through your salon, pointing out your choice of product lines, signature services, and specialists on your team. In smaller salons, this conversation may never leave the front of the salon, but still introduces the new client to who you are and what you have to offer.

5. Scripts for Success

Consistency is the key to success when creating a successful front desk team. Create a script book of "Hollywood lines" for your front desk person. This will create consistency and ease the training process. Topics to include for your scripts are: the phone greeting, welcoming the client, confirmation calls, new client calls, "wake-up" calls, opening the sale, closing the sale, pre-booking, and offering additional services.

6. Systems for Success

OPENING THE SALE FOR ADD-ON SERVICES AND RETAIL – Train your front desk team to understand how to maximize the schedule and learn how to grow the service providers. The front desk should have a strategy on how to fill openings on the book.

- Confirmation call
- Greeting the client

- Salon tours
- "Wake-up" calls (clients who are due, but have not yet scheduled their appointment)

CLOSING THE EXPERIENCE WITH TEAM SYNERGY & THE SERVICE TICKET – Use the service ticket as a resource for team communication. The service provider should write when the client needs to come back in and what products were recommended on the service ticket.

GOALS – Implementing a goal and reward system is essential for motivating, tracking, and coaching/mentoring the individuals on your front desk team. Each goal should reflect the principles/targets of growing the salon business through the front desk. The goals should be customized according to your current business trends, but be high enough to establish proper growth of your salon. Don't forget goals for these five profit principles:

- Pre-booking
- Referrals
- Additional services
- Retail
- Gift cards

7. Rewards

Implementing a goal system also requires the follow-through of a reward program. Rewards should be given monthly according to the accomplishment of the goals. Since there are five goals, there should be five levels of monthly rewards. In order to stay within budget of front desk salaries, we recommend the goals start at $15 for a level one reward and go as high as a paid day off for hitting five goals in one month.

8. Tracking

Each individual should track their daily progress on their efforts to hit their goals. This will effectively track the sales in the success principles of additional services, gift card sales, referrals, pre-booking, and retail. Tracking provides the salon owner the opportunity to visually see the efforts and hold the front desk individuals accountable in using their sales training, and scripts in making service and retail offerings.

9. Coaching & Mentoring

Salon owners or managers need to plan 30-minute meetings with each individual on the front desk team. Review tracking and make suggestions on scripts or actions to teach front desk team members how to hit goals.

10. Salon Team Meetings

Monthly team meetings are essential for a healthy, strong team culture. During the salon meetings, celebrate the front desk efforts and success. Refer to the tracking sheets to quantify the efforts the front desk has made in building the salon business and service providers. Acknowledge individual goals achieved and pass out rewards at the meeting.

CHAPTER 36

The Transition—The Controversial Exit

"Unless you try to do something beyond what you have already mastered, you will never grow."

—Ronald E. Osborn

I t's time. You just signed a lease after many weeks of negotiating and reviewing all your projections. What do you do if you are currently working in another salon because you need the income you are producing?

- How do you transition?

- When do you tell the salon owner?

- Do you tell your current employer and hope for the best?

- When do you tell your clients?

- How do you hire your staff?

- When do you start promoting your salon?

This chapter will guide you through all of these questions and give you suggestions and things to consider.

If you are thinking about your transition out of your current job, then that means the lease is done and you need to start planning your business model. If your salon won't be ready for four to six months because of construction, then we recommend that you tell NO ONE! Of course, discuss everything with your significant other or business partner going in on the business, but other than that, tell no one.

We have seen many hairdressers tell a few of their clients and, after a few weeks, a client may slip and say something to the salon owner or another hairdresser. Believe it or not, the average person only picks up 11 percent of a person's conversation.

You can talk to your clients and quietly gather their email addresses and telephone numbers. Don't tell them about "the new salon," just let them know you are updating your files and contact information for future promotions. Be discreet. If the salon owner sees you collecting this information, he or she will get suspicious. Also, if it's a color client, make notes on their formula.

If your salon is close to your existing workplace, we recommend that you put paper in the windows in the front of the store, keep your front door locked, and have your construction crew use the back entrance. If the salon owner you work for suspects competition, he or she will stop by to see who is opening up, what services they are offering, and snoop around to find out as much as possible. You want to be very strategic and stay hidden as long as possible. It's only natural that your current salon owner will want to find out the competing salon in their backyard.

You do not want your owner to walk into the location while it's under construction; they might tell a construction worker or the general contractor that they're looking for work and would like to get in touch with the new owner. The crew may not realize the implications and say your name or give your telephone number because they think they are helping you to get a new employee. The owner can research the county or the state and find out who may be opening; so, make the mailing address a post office box number or your attorney's office.

When do you tell the current salon owner? We have seen many stylists tell the salon owner months in advance about opening their own salon. Since they felt more like a friend than an employee, they mistakenly thought that the owner would be very happy for them. Unless the salon is located more than 20 miles away, you become a threat to your employer. In most cases, you will be immediately fired.

The next thing you know, you are trying to scramble to find a place to work and keep your existing clientele. The salon owner will try to take your clients away from you, not tell them where you have gone, book them with another stylist, and keep as many of your clients as possible. So, you need to tell your employer when you are prepared to leave. Whenever possible, wait until the last minute. They may say, "Stay until you are open." But, in most cases, you are not only the competition, but you will take your clients and possibly other stylists or providers with you. Be very careful.

When do you tell your fellow stylists? It is a very difficult question. Again, if you are months away from opening, tell no one. Your news will leak out if the "wrong" person overhears a conversation about what you are doing. The next thing you know, you will be called into the owner's office and fired. You can put your whole plan in jeopardy if you are let go from your current, income-producing job before you are ready. We would wait until you are a few weeks from opening and prepared to leave before saying anything.

How do you hire your staff? The first person you need to hire and look for is your front desk professional or a salon manager. That person will help you hire and keep you out of the limelight before you open. There will be a lot of tasks that need to be done before you open. This person will be very helpful while you are still working to produce revenue. It is very important that you get along with this person, have the same philosophy, and understand the path and the culture you want to create.

The front desk professional or salon manager is an investment. As soon as you hire this person, they are going to want a salary. Try to be creative with them, but figure it into your budget. Now, you are ready to look for staff.

You can solicit stylists from other salons, but be careful. In a small town or when your salon is in close proximity to your existing salon, gossip spreads like a bad fire. It is always great to bring someone on board with a full book, but be careful of the commission they are asking for.

Another way to hire your staff is to go to an industry school to find them. L'Oreal-affiliated schools offer excellent education and are a viable source for finding newly trained students. First, find the school, get to know the manager, and find out the best students graduating. Bring in friends and family to try out the newly graduated student. If you feel this person does quality work, it's like finding a "diamond in the rough."

The best part in all of this is that new graduates will be open to understand and be receptive to the business culture and atmosphere you want to create. Also, you can start the student at 40 percent commission as an apprentice. Then, gradually work them up to a higher percentage after a 6-month period. Since new graduates don't have followings, it is important that you budget more money for marketing and advertising to get new clients into your salon.

Let's say you are opening a salon far away from your existing place of work. How do you find staff? Well, one way is to place postcards in all the strip malls that are close to your location, stating that you are opening and looking for stylists, colorists, nail techs, and massage therapists. You will get some phone calls; there are always people who are ready for a move or unhappy in their present salon for one reason or another.

Although it may seem like a good idea at first, going into a busy salon to seek out and lure the superstars away from their current job and salon is not advisable. Just like you have a dream of salon ownership, your fellow salon owners have that same dream. Find ways to attract job seekers to you, rather than hunting them down and pulling them from other salons. Acquiring people this way can lead to a slew of problems. If you think of someone coming into your salon and pulling away the people that you've invested in and worked hard to acquire, you would be upset and angry.

Do the hard work to find qualified candidates; it will pay off. Stick with schools, word-of-mouth, print classifieds, and online classifieds as well.

Craigslist is a great place to start with online classifieds. If you look on Craigslist right now, you will find a ton of ads for beauty salon employment. It's recommended that you create an email that is just for use with your Craigslist account and employment ads. Unfortunately, the one issue with Craigslist is the amount of spam that you will receive. Regardless, it is still a great way to place free ads about your salon's job openings.

April Levesque Ducker

"[My boss] found out before we gave our notice and changed the locks—she didn't take it so well!

I feel as though it's a natural progression within the field and vowed to myself that I will not react poorly when the time comes for me. I am sure it's very difficult, but (like parenting) I will do my best not to take it personally."

CHAPTER 37

The Open House

"You have to dream before your dreams can come true."
—Abdul Kalam

The big day is finally happening and all your efforts are about to become reality. Let friends, family, neighbors, and future clients know that you are going to be open for business. An open house or grand opening celebration provides you and your staff the ability to showcase and reach many new people in your area—many of whom have no idea that a new salon is opening in their town. The event will allow you to let people know exactly what your salon will offer from a service and product standpoint. The event will also allow you to have some fun, reveal your personality, and let everyone feel at home.

The reason behind an open house is to create a buzz, show people you are different, and generate excitement for your company. The salon has to be 100 percent finished and your staff ready and dressed for success.

The key to a successful open house is the preparation beforehand. Follow these basic steps to ensure that your new salon's event is a smash.

Identify Your Audience

Determine what type of clients you would like to attract and your target audience for your open house. Sit down with your staff and decide on how many family and friends each of you will invite. Once decided, that will give you an indication of how many people you can invite and if you can handle that amount. You can then tailor the guest list to add additional people, neighboring businesses, local schools, local sports teams, town officials, and organizational leaders.

Create a Budget

You should have a budget for your open house—stay under your budget if you can. The expected cost for an open house will be close to $2000 if at least 100 people attend. As you will discover, unexpected expenses will occur during the first few months of business. Going overboard on your event is not a wise thing to do. The first thing to determine is how many people you have invited. It may seem like a huge amount of people. You can estimate that five to ten percent of the people you invite will actually attend the open house. That is a reasonable number of people to expect on top of family and friends.

Your new business will have to absorb each facet of the open house. You may even have to factor in parking attendants or additional staff to help greet people. Following are a number of items that you should figure into your event budget.

Food & Beverage

Vegetable tray, fruit tray, small sandwiches, pastries, cheese tray, soda, wine, coffee, and tea.

Miscellaneous Expenses

Balloons, flowers, newspaper advertisements, flyer advertisements, salon menus, postage for a mailer, and tables/chair rentals.

Giveaways

Shampoo samples, water bottles, pens, magnetic business cards, and/or T-shirts.

Choose the Date & Time

Every open house should offer guests a window of time to drop in and visit. The event should last no longer than four hours. Doing so enables your invited guests to visit at their leisure. Weekends, late afternoon, and evening hours are good times for an open house. Your guests will have conflicts with work and family any other time. When choosing a date, make sure it is not a holiday or a time of the year when the weather is bad. Plan your opening and event in a month that has milder weather.

Advertise

To get people to your door, you must advertise effectively. Flyers, print ads in the local newspaper, penny savers, and postcard mailings are a direct way to target your area. You should also post signs in local businesses for your open house. Many local magazines may allow you to post your event at no charge in their upcoming "events" area of the magazine. You can also post your event online through news websites at no charge. Your local paper might also allow you to post an event free of charge in that section. Posting a large sign about the open house on your store window is an effective way to create a buzz in the neighborhood and let people know you are opening.

If you decide to run a print ad in your paper or send out invitations, you should include directions so people can find you easily. Also let people know that you will give away products. People love giveaways and a free bite to eat—that alone should stir some interest and get people to your salon opening.

You should also have a product and service menu available the night of your open house. If you and your staff are busy—and, hopefully, you will be—it is important that people who come to the event leave with the menu of services and a price list of products offered at your new salon.

Getting Ready for Opening Day

A few days before the event, prepare your staff for their function and roles. Have a dry run on how you would like things to go. Establish who will greet people. Most importantly, establish a list of everyone attending. A good idea is to have a sign-in book with space for name, phone, address, and email. If you want to be more creative, have someone greet your open house guests with a laptop or tablet PC in hand. Collect their personal information, while they sip on a beverage. It may also make sense to establish where you want your staff to be stationed. If you are offering demonstrations, you should not have your staff crowded around, but standing close by to answer questions.

The most important thing is planning to book future appointments. You should have someone at your front desk at all times greeting people, explaining the services the salon will offer, and booking appointments. Your staff should be well-rehearsed on this. All should understand that this is the focus of the event. It should be easy to get your staff's family and friends to book appointments. Focus on the new people in the crowd and clients who are making the transition with you. You may even want your front desk staff to offer a special discount to those who book an appointment during the open house.

Once the event commences, mingle with the guests. Take a few moments to introduce yourself and your staff, describe your business, and personally thank everyone who has attended.

Plan to have a ribbon-cutting ceremony when the salon has the most guests. Have all of your staff involved for the cutting of the ribbon. If possible, have a town official cut the ribbon. That will signify the official opening of your business. It would be a great idea to let the local newspapers know of your event so that they can be present for pictures. Contact them well in advance so they have time to put your event on their schedules. Finally, be sure to write a press release, distribute it through a press release distribution service, and post it on your website.

CHAPTER 38

Buying an Existing Salon

It's often said that buying a salon is easier than starting one from scratch. Everything is done—the burden of buying equipment, salon design, staff, and signage is complete. You can leave your current job, start running the salon, and make money almost immediately.

As a forewarning, this might all sound good, but many businesses are sold because they have inherent problems that prevent them from generating sufficient income. The behind-the-scene problems are very difficult to see as an outsider. If you are considering buying a business, it is vital that you conduct a comprehensive research and analysis, as if you were setting the business up from the beginning yourself.

First Steps

The first step is to decide what type of salon you want to be. Will you concentrate on color, cuts, and will you offer any spa-type services? That should quickly narrow down what salons are available that may be of interest to you.

The next thing you should look at is the size of the business you want. Bigger salons mean bigger challenges, like larger rent, staff management, and expenses. You also must consider the location. Are you prepared to move and/or travel daily to work? Travel time to and from home will quickly cut into valuable family time and make what you thought was a smart investment into a very expensive mistake.

What to Look for in a Business

The first thing to look for is time in business under the same ownership. If the salon has been there over five years, they most likely have worked out all the nuances of a startup business. They should also have a decent staff and good stream of customers. The most common mistake people make is when they buy a business outside of their expertise. Think long and hard about the skill level and knowledge of the existing staff at the location of interest. Will the existing staff meet your expectations or will you need to let some go and hire replacements? If you are young and progressive, you may not want to look at a salon close to a retirement area.

NOTE

When buying an existing salon, the culture is in place and it may be difficult in the beginning to instill your philosophy.

Remember to investigate the level of competition facing the business. Is this the reason they are selling? Is a young, cool, slick salon on the next block taking away customers daily? Make sure you know your potential competitors' strengths and weaknesses relative to the business you may buy. An area with several salons close by may not be a good investment, especially in a town that may not grow any more. Competition keeps you on your toes, but it's not good if you can't get your share of the market.

Location, Location, Location! We have all heard this before. This is the single most important part of your purchase. Ensure that the business is located in an area that is close to the audience you want to attract and in reach of appropriately skilled employees. A salon in a small town may limit customers and staff. Bigger cities and a location close to a beauty school will certainly make it easier to attract new customers and staff.

Capital requirements are another issue. You must calculate how much you need for an overhaul, including: new furniture and equipment, a new floor, new paint, new ceiling, or a technology boost. That should be deducted from the asking price. Going in with blinders on is not a smart move. A simple, quick face-lift could easily run well over $10,000.

Putting a Price Tag on the Business

It may be useful to hire a business appraiser or a financial advisor when putting a value on an existing salon or business. The appraiser would be able to assist you in putting an estimated value on the business you are looking to purchase. To value a business, appraisers and advisors use three methods: the asset value, earnings multiple, and return on capital.

Asset Value

It is not an easy task to put a finger on exactly what a business is worth. The net asset value (net worth), is determined by taking whatever liabilities/financial obligations exist (outstanding debts, loan repayments, outstanding invoices, and business credit card balances) and subtracting it from the value of the assets. The value for the entire business will be the net asset value, plus a value for good will, representing the reputation of the business and existing clientele.

In the salon business, you must also determine how important the previous owner is to the business. If he or she is the leading generator of income in the salon and they plan to leave the business, their departure will considerably reduce the asset value. It may be a good idea to get a noncompete agreement against the owner if they are leaving.

You should get one even if the owner is staying. They may not like the way you operate or manage and leave unexpectedly.

Earnings Multiple

The earnings multiple method requires you to apply a multiple to the earnings from the business. Earnings should take into account interest charges to be paid after purchasing the business and any loans needed to make improvements.

Here is the formula: divide the company's market price by its after-tax earnings over a one-year period. The calculations should give you an idea if the salon is overpriced or not. To make this easy to understand, if there is a small amount of after-tax earnings and the salon needs a face-lift, your earnings multiple will be very small. The salon is not worth very much at all.

Return on Capital

To find the return on capital (monies used to purchase the salon), you will need to define a desired rate of return on the monies you have invested to purchase the salon business. The rate of return can be defined as a ratio of profit made from monies you invested in a bank, in a CD, or money market, over a year's term. That money will be used to purchase the salon.

The income of the business before interest and tax should be calculated over a one-year period. If the percentage is higher than your return from the bank or any monies used for the purchase of the salon, then you are off to a great start and sound investment.

The return on capital is sometimes not important to all new potential business owners. Is this business a dream of yours or a labor of love? Is this something you have always wanted to do or are you are buying this business for or from a family member? Whatever the case, realize that it may take a bit longer before the business starts to make money and pay you back your full investment and proper dividends.

Go With Your Gut

Finally, you can always get an accountant or financial advisor involved—one who can really dissect a business when you are looking to make a purchase. Their knowledge of finances and the salon business will be more than helpful when determining if you should or shouldn't go ahead with this purchase. We do believe you should not buy a business without their help.

Let's start with a large cup of your favorite coffee. Cancel all appointments for the next three days. Drive to the salon that you are evaluating for purchase. Arrive at the opening of the salon and sit quietly in your car without being noticed. Take notes on what time staff and customers start to arrive.

Check off the questions below as you answer them.

- ○ Who gets there first?
- ○ Is it busy?
- ○ What type of people work in the area?
- ○ Is there plenty of parking?
- ○ Is there potential for new business?
- ○ Is the salon an important part of the business community where it is located?
- ○ Is there room for growth?

Do this for three days. Make it fun. Look at it as your opportunity to be a private-eye investigator or a detective. Your goal is to go undetected and find out as much information as possible. Get there at different times each day; sit for a few hours. We can guarantee that your gut will tell you if this business is something you should buy. You want to ensure that you are spending your hard-earned money well and investing in a business that you can grow and enjoy for many years to come.

Make It Happen

Are you ready to look under the hood of this business? You will need to let your intentions be known to the owner and obtain the business information that you need to make a final assessment of the numbers. The information needed will be a copy of the lease, name of the landlord, vendor information, copies of all monthly expenses, and an employee list, along with compensation breakdown for each employee. The most important piece of information is a detailed list of customers, dating back as long as possible.

The make-it-happen stage of purchasing a business is when you break down each area of the business you may purchase. You will need to look at the strengths, weaknesses, opportunities, and threats on this potential purchase.

Look at the current position of the salon in its market, its past performance, and its potential for growth. Look at its available resources, money, and manpower (stylists/service providers). Good cosmetologists are hard to find and keep. Interview the staff currently working in the salon. Will they fit your business structure? You will also need to consider whether the existing staff is suitable for the business and how they will react to a new owner.

Check to see what products the salon is currently using. Will the products used in the salon meet your expectations? Are they sold in neighboring salons?

Find out who the competition is, where they are, and what makes the salon different than the other competing salons in the area. Will the current clients stay aboard when you transition the salon after the previous owner moves on? Client loyalty is a must.

Determine a Purchase Price

The asking price for anything is never cast in stone. The person selling the business will be very attached to the business. Selling it will be a very emotional experience for them. Remember, they have probably built this business from scratch with many hours, months, and years of sweat equity. How do you give them an offer that doesn't insult them and put them on the defense?

You will need to put a value on the business. Once your homework has been done, breaking down each segment should give you a number that you can live with for a respectable offer. The key to making an offer is having everything broken down on paper. You can explain to the owner how you came up with your offer. Going in without a detailed breakdown being unprepared is a big mistake. Having this detailed list in front of you will open up discussions about things the owner may not have realized. Make a few copies of this information that you can leave with the seller if you have not consummated a deal.

Bottom-Line Number

You should have a bottom-line number going into negotiations—before you make an offer. It will enable you to negotiate effectively and not pay more than you can afford or are willing to pay. The seller may state an asking price outright, at which time you may or may not be prepared to negotiate.

Big Mistakes Buyers Make—Do Your Due Diligence

Without thorough research, you may find that you have made a terrible mistake six months into new ownership. A view of any business prospect can be easily distorted and misleading. You don't want to get attached before you find out the real facts, figures, and forecasts.

We have a very important rule of thumb when buying a home or business—never get emotionally attached. Learn to walk away from an opportunity when everything doesn't seem quite right. Moving to the next opportunity can save you a tremendous amount of time, money, and effort.

William J. Thompson Jr.

"Keeping the staff of the existing salon we bought. In an effort to make the transition smooth and not cause a big scene when we took over, we kept the staff on good faith rather than interview them ourselves. Within 6 months, we had to fire them all for various reasons."

Patty Hardy

"Catering to the gals who were already there. They rented and I didn't want to lose them. As soon as I got the tools I needed, I started running my salon the way I wanted to. Had a big walk-out and it was the best thing that ever happened. I refilled the salon with an incredible team, and had a few of the past gals ask to come back—of course, I said no."

CHAPTER 39

Booth Renting

This chapter will talk about either renting a booth or owning a booth-renting salon. Booth renting has not been around for a very long time. It only became an organized type of business about 15 years ago. There are several types of booth-renting operations:

Booth-Rental Salon With All Private Rooms

A salon with booths for rent is the "Beverly Hills" of booth renting. Each stylist has their own studio that is a complete "mini-salon" with a washbasin, styling station, dryer, and phone system with a computer for booking appointments. The cosmetologist (massage therapist, nail tech, colorist, etc.) has their first opportunity to become an entrepreneur, without the costs or management of owning a salon.

When you work at a salon, there are benefits you may not realize. If you have a large booking and are busy all the time, there are added expenses and responsibilities that you have to address as a business owner:

- Booking your own appointments
- Cleaning your space
- Shampooing clients
- Paying bills
- Ordering product
- Opening and closing
- Answering your own phone

Be prepared to buy products as a startup cost. Plus, we strongly recommend that you put together a retail product case for your clients—that is added revenue. Each rental location is different as far as the services they offer. Some book appointments for you, others have a café, retail center, and boutique in the lobby.

The most important factor is the rent you are going to pay, so we advise you to do your projections before you commit to a lease to see if it pays to leave your present workplace. You might be a person that makes 60 percent commission, which is fantastic for you. In this case, the salon owner is not making much and it may not pay to leave. The most positive thing in booth renting is you are your own boss; you can come and go as you please and book yourself out whenever you want.

Creating Your Own Booth Renting Operation

Creating a booth-renting salon is not the standard practice in the industry, but seems to be growing across the country. We have seen several successful operations and understand how to create a profitable salon environment if you decide to go in this direction. Let us give you a brief breakdown of startup costs and equipment needed to open this type of salon:

1. Construction

- Increased electric (several outlets in each room)
- Increased plumbing (a sink in every room, upgraded hot water system)
- Communication wiring (computer, phone, credit card, alarm)
- Air conditioning (extensive ductwork to each room)
- Drywall (building "multiple mini-salons" in one space)
- Flooring (more durable flooring and installation costs)
- Increased lighting (adequate lighting in each room)
- Bathrooms (multiple, larger for increased traffic)
- Painting (much more detail)
- Carpentry
- Break room/laundry room

2. Equipment

- Sinks or backwash units in every room
- Dryer chair for every room
- Reception chair for every room
- Hydraulic chair for every room
- Storage cabinets for every room
- Workstation for every room
- Front reception desk

3. Costs

- Upfront construction much more expensive
- Equipment costs more expensive
- Deposits for rent are larger (bigger space needed)
- Legal fees are higher (contracts needed for renters)
- Larger insurance premiums
- Salary for manager or front desk professionals

The booth-rental salon allows you to be a salon owner without dealing with the nuisances of running and managing staff. In this case, you are a landlord and become responsible for your tenants. The tenants are the cosmetologists who rent space from you. Although this may seem much easier, you still will have a huge responsibility to your tenants and their clients.

Other things to be aware of as a booth-rental salon owner:

- Once you are at 100% capacity (fully rented), your income is capped
- Expenses go up when renting (electric, water, gas)
- Turnover is higher than a normal salon
- Maintenance costs are much greater
- Hours of operation are longer

Startup costs for a salon rental operation vary greatly. In Chapter 5 (Negotiating With the Landlord), we noted that startup costs can have a big impact on your ability to turn a profit quickly. Work on negotiating with the landlord to pay for some or all of the build-out for your location. Also, negotiating a good rental agreement will give you time to get tenants (cosmetologists) to occupy your space.

Open Booth Renting—No Rooms

A salon like this is set up like your traditional salon. It may look like a normal operation and your customers may not know the difference. Most of the time, all expenses are paid by the salon owner, unless the owner has a program to pay the shampoo assistant and product costs. In some salons, they have lockers located at the shampoo area and you use your own products. Everyone splits the cost of the shampoo assistant. In this type of rental salon, the cost to rent is usually a lot less than the one listed above.

> **NOTE**
> You are renting a normal styling station, not a room.

Owning the salon and renting it out has good and bad points. The positive is that your overhead is covered and you, as the owner, are behind the chair making a good income while the rest of the salon covers all expenses and puts some money into your pocket.

The negative is that your income revenue is set and limited to what you make. If some renters leave, your income can be reduced dramatically and quickly. All of a sudden, you are paying a lot of the bills with your revenue because the rental of booths is not covering all the expenses for your salon.

Every situation is different, but the bottom line is to do your projections and see what your profits could be. By doing your homework, you can make a decision going into the situation and business opportunity with your eyes open, understanding the costs and potential revenue.

In the booth-rental ownership situation, most salons need to be larger to accommodate more stations or rooms. However, make sure that you don't choose a bigger space if the business doesn't warrant it. You can always start smaller and expand when you have developed a sound operation.

Salon Owner/Operators Discuss the Good, the Bad, & the Ugly

Keisa Stewart-Rucker

"[Not] setting the rules for the booth renters!"

Francis Greis, Kure Beach, North Carolina – Downtown Hair

"I set up bylaws that my tenants sign and must live by. They must keep their space clean and respect all property and customers of others. If they don't, I ask them to leave. Bad tenants make it difficult for others to do business."

CHAPTER 40

The Facelift—Remodeling Your Existing Salon

"The road to success is always under construction."

—Lily Tomlin

Remodel Your Salon & Change Your Image

This might be the best time to start planning an image upgrade and a salon remodel. Many things have changed in the way we conduct business in the salon environment. The once-loyal customer is looking to better manage work and family through value, better customer service, and the ability to shop closer to home. These changes in the way people do business will have far-reaching effects that won't disappear overnight.

The marketing of your salon, your budgeting skills, and how you manage customers and staff has to adapt for business survival. You can't expect your business to thrive and do well without changing yourself. The current appearance of your salon may look dated, tired, and even dirty to your clients. Once your salon reaches this point, it may be too late. The longer you wait to make changes the more it will cost you in construction and improvements to catch up to your competition.

While the thought of investing in a remodel can be overwhelming, don't let your fears get the best of you. If things are slow, use this time to focus on your salon remodel and new image for your salon business.

Cost, Budget, & Value

You have committed to moving forward with the project, but how do you figure out what you want to spend? How much will it cost to move a wall, rip out the old floor, and buy all new furniture and equipment? What should you expect to spend? How do you set an appropriate budget? How long should you expect to take before all this pays you back? How can you maximize your return on investment?

This section lays out the foundation and factors that will influence how much to spend on your build-out and salon furniture/equipment.

Cost

Breaking it down to the simplest terms, the cost is a function of the materials you will need for your build-out, the time, the labor for the contractors to complete the work, and the new equipment and furniture you will be purchasing.

Budget

We all want the best of everything, but most of us have champagne tastes with a beer budget. Your list of needs and wants may exceed your ability to foot the bill. While the cost of the renovation will vary due to many different things, like how extensive the remodel and what type of furniture/equipment you choose, you still have to establish a budget.

Deciding on your budget is based on some critical information. Generally, it depends on your demographics, how much you charge for services, and what type of clients your salon attracts. You also need to know what you can afford as a monthly payment if financing is needed. You should factor in what you have put aside in cash for the project.

Return on Investment

How do you know if your investment is going to pay off? How long will it take to recoup your remodeling dollars?

There is a particular rule of thumb for return on investment in remodeling your salon business. Statistics show that normally you can expect an increase of business of about 20 percent in the first year of your remodel. This increase would come from new customers that have never visited your salon before the remodel.

Your current staff and existing clients will have the benefit of working at and visiting the hottest salon in the area. The fact that you are keeping your current clientele and not losing staff to competitors down the street is a big factor you must weigh into your calculations when figuring your overall return on investment.

What's Your Budget?

There are many ways to change the look of a salon. The cost does not have to be in the tens of thousands. Whether your budget is $1000, $20,000, or $100,000, most changes will significantly increase business within the first year of the remodel. These will keep your salon looking fresh and ahead of your competition. Your customers will appreciate it and so will your staff.

Remodeling Your Salon on a Tight Budget

Mr. Clean

The best way to make your salon look fresh and give it a new look is with a deep clean. Roll up your sleeves and put on a fresh set of gloves and get down to business or hire a commercial cleaning service. We suggest that you periodically hire a commercial cleaning service—whether it's once or twice a year or even once a quarter. They will get into every corner of your business and wipe away years of grime. This will give your salon a fresh appearance that your customer will notice. Plus, a nice fresh floor waxing will make any salon look new.

It's a "Bright" Light

Replace every bulb in your salon. Light levels in bulbs and florescent bulbs tend to be less bright or give off a brownish glare after a couple of years. Changing your bulbs will brighten up the way everything in your salon looks. Light brings life!

Bring in New Products

Changing your salon doesn't always have to be with a paint brush and a hammer. Bring in new products, change your shelving, and show your customers you are committed to the beauty industry by introducing them to cutting-edge beauty products.

Look Up

If your ceiling is dirty or has water stains, either give it a coat of paint or change out the stained ceiling tiles (we will talk more about ceiling tiles later in this chapter). The worst thing in the salon business is when you are getting your hair shampooed and you look up and see a water-stained ceiling. This is a sign of true neglect in a salon.

Your "Door" to Success

The first and last thing your staff and customers see when walking into your salon is your front door. Your front door should always be clean. If it is wood, give it a fresh coat of paint. If it's full glass, you may want to put your name, logo, and hours on the door. This is an inexpensive way to make a noticeable change.

The Big Remodel

Designer/Architect

To find out the costs of this endeavor, we recommend you bring in a specialist in the industry. Several companies specialize in salon layouts and salon furniture (see Chapter 11). They need to come to the salon, see what you want to change, and discuss the look you want to create. You will pay a design fee; but, if you are doing a complete makeover, we recommend it highly. They have the expertise and can give you advice on prioritizing your remodeling steps.

Contractors

Usually, you bring in a contractor only for extensive changes. But, every situation is different, depending on how much remodeling you want to do. You may only want to paint and change the floor. For this type of work, you may not need a general contractor. Take two steps: bring in a contractor and get a complete price on everything you want to do. Next, bring in separate subcontractors: a plumber, electrician, floor specialist, and a drywall team to get separate prices on your projects. That will give you an idea of costs.

If you are just replacing the salon furniture, your costs should be minimal.

Create a Spreadsheet

Below, is a spreadsheet with a sample of some of the types of costs you may incur for your remodel. We recommend you fill it out and get a complete breakdown of what you want to do. It is a good guideline to start seeing your costs and what you want to spend on your remodeling project.

Construction Breakdown		Furniture Breakdown	
Plumbing		Styling chairs	
Electrical		Dryer chairs	
Drywall		Shampoo units	
Painting		Shampoo cabinet	
Flooring		Pedicure chairs	
Construction demolition		Manicure stations	
Signage		Stools	
Telephone		Styling stations	
Computer		Color stations	
Window treatment		Color chairs	
Furniture installation		Dispensary	
Furniture demolition		Color lab	
Architect's plans		Reception desk	
Permits		Makeup unit	

(Spreadsheet is continued on next page)

(Spreadsheet is continued from previous page)

Construction Breakdown		Furniture Breakdown	
		Retail area	
		Reception furniture	
TOTAL		**TOTAL**	

Painting Changes the Look With a Small Price Tag

When opening a salon or remodeling an existing one, you will be faced with a major obstacle. What is the first thing you should do that fits your budget, but will have the biggest impact?

Of course, you want to rip out everything and start from scratch. We all want to have the best of everything when we own a business. The fact is that you just might not be able to afford it.

What is the one thing that can instantly and affordably change the look and appearance of your salon once it is done? The answer is new, fresh paint. The best part about painting is that you don't always have to hire a professional to do the work. Most of us are capable of painting. It's usually easy to find family, friends, and maybe a few employees to assist with the project.

Consider changing the colors. We write about colors in your salon in Chapter 21. Changing the color will give you and your clients the greatest sense of immediate change and satisfaction. Follow these tips to decrease the effort and cost involved with painting:

- Make sure you have enough drop cloths to cover everything.
- Tape off places that you do not want to get paint on. (It will take a while to do but cleanup of unwanted paint takes hours.)
- Buy enough paint. (You don't want to run out in the middle of the project to buy more paint.)
- Make sure you buy paint you can wipe and clean (semi-gloss, eggshell finish).
- Paint the ceilings first, then the walls.
- Don't buy cheap brushes and rollers.
- Use a top-grade paint.

If painting is not your thing and you just don't have the time, hire it out. You can search on Google and/or Yahoo for painters in your area. Listed below are the two most popular websites to find painters:

www.localpainterquotes.com

www.paintingnetworx.com

How Painters Determine What They Charge

Commercial painting contractors use several aspects to determine the formula for your project. The cheapest price you will get is on an empty space that is new construction; the most expensive is on an older building and/or restoration project. These factors listed below will help you understand.

- How much salon furniture do they have to move?
- Do they have to work at night and around your schedule?
- How many windows and doors do they have to paint?
- How high are the ceilings? The higher the ceilings, the higher the quote. They will need ladders and scaffolding.
- Do you need a primer to cover old paint and stains?
- What type of repairs do they have to make to your walls?
- Trim (woodworking is measured by the linear foot for painting).
- Overall size of your space.

Ceiling Tiles

Changing ceiling tiles can be a quick fix and make the salon look new with a good paint job. Among residential ceiling choices, drop ceiling tiles is a preferred option. These are durable tiles and need little maintenance. However, drop ceiling tiles may develop a worn-out look over time. In such a scenario, you need to paint them. Ceiling tiles should be removed with care to ensure that they are not damaged. Tiles that have cracked might need replacement. To remove, paint, and replace your drop ceiling tiles, use the following information:

Step 1—Removing Drop Ceiling Tiles

Position a ladder against the drop ceiling. Prepare yourself with plastic gloves. Drop ceiling tiles are set within a frame or a tiling grid. Removing the tile without due care can harm the edges of the tile, making it unfit for reinstallation in its framework. The edges of the tile might be compacted with dust or grime. Use the tip of a flat screwdriver covered with cloth to scrape off the debris and push along the edges. Slightly push one end of the tile. You need to slide the tile along its frame. After pushing the tile forward, twist it to create an angle with the horizontal grid. Now, slide out the tile from its frame. If you find any loose wires, cover them with twist-on wire connectors or electrical tape.

Step 2—Examining Drop Ceiling Tile

Place the removed tile on a sheet of newspaper. Use a dry cloth to clean the tile. Examine the edges of the tile. If the edges are broken or if the surface of the tile is cracked in many places, you need to replace it. Otherwise, you can paint it.

Step 3—Painting Drop Ceiling Tile

Use a latex paint. You can use a paint roller or a paintbrush, depending upon the texture of the tile. Paint rollers are better for plain surfaces, while a brush helps to dab into the crevices of tiles with textured exteriors. Use a latex paint with a color matching the surrounding drop ceiling tiles. It is best to protect the edges of the tile with masking tape when painting it, as painted edges might hamper the fitting of the tile into its designated slot. Allow the painted tile to dry for a few hours.

Step 4—Purchasing Replacement Drop Ceiling Tiles

Replacement drop ceiling tiles are available at hardware supply stores. Further, you can also contact the retailer from whom you purchased the tiles to request a replacement. It is better to purchase a couple of tiles for future replacements. The existing drop ceiling tile design may get outdated so having reserve tiles is a wise option.

Step 5—Installing Replacement/Painted Drop Ceiling Tile

Carry your replacement/painted tile up the ladder. Hold it in such a way that the finished/painted side is facing downward. Tilt the tile upward and into the grid. Allow nearly half of the ceiling tile to pass the grid's frame. Now, start to position the tile in a horizontal manner, ensuring that the tile's edges are tightly fitted along the frame.

Getting Started, the Permit Way

If your salon is in operation, it is important to coordinate the remodel so you don't lose any business. If the job is large and permits are needed for the renovation, it is recommended that you do your remodel in stages.

For example, in changing your shampoo sinks, you need to pull out the old shampoo unit and cabinets, change the plumbing pipes, and install the new units. It is usually a two-day process. Once it's all done, then it's time to call the plumbing inspector in your city for inspection. Hopefully, the inspector will pass the plumbing work. If not, you can't use the sinks and won't be able to open until it is satisfactory to the inspector and is compliant to all county or city codes. That is just one inspection! What if you are trying to coordinate several inspections? It is a very difficult task. In this case, you are hiring a general contractor and it's his responsibility to make sure everything is done on time. The key is to tell him your priorities and let him coordinate these tasks with his subcontractors. Timing is everything.

Priorities—Plumbing

The shampoo area is a very important department in a salon. Without being able to wash a person's hair color out or just to shampoo someone's head, your salon cannot function. You have to be efficient and work with a structured timeline for any makeovers or remodels to this area because without this department, your salon cannot reopen.

Most salons close Saturday evening and reopen Tuesday for business, so it is important to have all of your furniture on hand or have your equipment supplier deliver for Saturday evening or Sunday morning. You probably will pay a premium for this service; but, in most cases, you will have no choice. First, you must tear out the old cabinets and sink units. If you are remodeling the dispensary and any pedicure units, all of this must be taken out as well.

Then, the installation begins. To install cabinets, such as a three-sink shampoo cabinet, the time it takes to professionally install it is 4 hours. Right behind that person will be a plumber to hook up all of the sinks. The average time to hook up each one is 1–3 hours, depending on the type. A freestanding sink unit and chair usually takes the longest. They must be bolted to the floor securely, which is the responsibility of the plumber. If he is a "one-man band," it could take a day and a half to secure and install three units, so be prepared.

Here is a list of equipment and furniture with the length of time and cost to install (averages):

- Wall sink (cabinet installed by others)—1½ hours, including mounting the bracket: $100 each

- Freestanding backwash sink—4 hours on average with bolting the unit to the floor: $250

- Pedicure Unit K—3 hours to install and assemble: $250

- Color lab sink or dispensary sink—1½ hours to install: $175

- Facial room sink installation—$150

- Remodel existing bathroom—labor is $400 for new fixture installation

These costs will help you estimate your construction budget. Prices may vary depending on the city or state you live in.

These prices do not reflect any changes in your plumbing, such as adding another sink or moving all the hot and cold water lines over to accommodate another sink unit.

Hiring the Subcontractors

You are getting ready to remodel and have brought in an electrician, plumber, and a drywall contractor. How do you know they are charging a fair price? It is a very tricky situation, because you want a great price and you are on a very tight budget. How do you handle this?

Our rule of thumb is to bring in two to three tradesmen from the same field and have them bid on the same work. Have a complete checklist to hand to them for the bid. Let them know that it might be weekend work or in the evenings, so that they price it accordingly. Plumbers and electricians get anywhere from $30 to $75 per hour, and on the weekends, maybe more. There may be a crew of two to three or just one. Get a complete price without the hourly breakdown. There are always some unforeseen situations and having a package deal is in your favor.

If you have three bids and two are about the same and one is considerably lower, you should be concerned. You may want to choose the lowest bidding contractor, but be careful! They either did not include something or did not charge enough for labor. The contractor might be the type that is spread very thin so your remodel will not be finished in a timely fashion. We would also check their references and recent work. See if they finished on time and on budget.

Permits—Plumbing

If permits are needed, here is the process. (Closing Saturday night – reopen Tuesday)

1. On Friday, call for a plumbing inspection with the city or county for Monday afternoon.
2. On Friday, deliver all new equipment/furniture concerning plumbing. If you don't have the room, pay a premium to get it delivered on Sunday morning. It depends on your salon space.
3. On Saturday—early evening—demolish all plumbing needed for the change.
4. On Sunday morning, bring in your cabinet company to install all furniture concerning plumbing.
5. Mid-Sunday morning, have your plumber come in and start prep work on all plumbing fixtures.
6. By noon Monday, the plumber finishes and you should be ready for the inspector.
7. By Tuesday morning, you will have passed inspection and reopened.

Priorities—Electric

Your electrical design in your newly bought salon could give you a few surprises, but not if you've read this chapter. One item that is often overlooked is the amount of power coming into your salon or the amount of amperage going to each styling station or other departments. Here are standards used in the industry:

- Styling station: Each station should have 10 amps of power with two stations on a 20-amp circuit breaker.
- Dryer chair: Each dryer (behind-the-chair style) generally draws 8 amps, and it should have two dryers per 20-amp circuit.
- Pedicure unit: This unit needs 20 amps on a ground fault interrupter (GFI) outlet.
- Nail table: Each table should have 5 amps or two tables on a 10-amp circuit.
- Reception desk: Recommended power for computers, credit card terminal, and miscellaneous items is 20 amps.
- Color station: Not much power needed there; GFI outlet would be useful.
- Color lab: Utility outlet and power for accessory lighting.

- Retail area: This can vary, but with several retail units, 30-amp circuits are recommended for lighting.

- Dispensary: Power for the washer, dryer, and hot water heater; these units usually need 220 volt power and require a lot of amperage. (Consult with your electrician.)

If you don't plan your electric properly, you will have circuit breakers tripping when stylists are in the middle of providing services to their clients. You can only run so many appliances on one circuit before it overloads and trips. To avoid this problem, bring in an electrician and show him what you want to have done. If you are changing the styling stations, show him the new design. In many cases, the electrical is in the wrong spot and has to be moved. Ask your salon design specialist to lay out your new stations with the current electrical setup in mind. You might not have to make any changes if you can work with what is already there and how it is currently wired.

Cost Breakout

Unless the salon owner is knowledgeable in electrical systems, the installation of outlets is not to be considered a "Do-it-Yourself" project. This is particularly true if new circuits need to be added to the electrical panel. Traditionally, installation is done by a professionally licensed electrician.

The costs for a project will include:

- Bringing electrical wiring and lighting to code: This is going to depend upon the amount of work required, but an electrician's average rate is from $65 to $85 per hour. Any given project might be priced on a per item basis or the electrician might simply craft a bid based on the number of tasks to be performed. Generally, it is recommended to have an electrician perform several installations on the same project to make it more cost effective.

- Installing standard outlets of 120 volts: Takes less than half an hour and usually costs around $100 each.

- Installing heavy-duty outlets of 220 to 240 volts: Takes less than half an hour and usually costs around $100 each.

- Installing grounded outlets for kitchens, bathrooms, and any places near water or moisture: Takes less than an hour and usually costs around $120 each.

> **NOTE**
>
> Remember, all fixtures that you use must be UL (Underwriter's Laboratory) approved.

- Installing a new circuit on the electrical panel and running the appropriate amount of conduit to the new location: This might take up to a full hour's time and costs around $185 each.

- Upgrading panel for heavy-duty outlets: Involves adding a 220 to 240-volt circuit, running conduit, and installing receptacle; this can take several hours and tends to cost around $650 for each addition.

Following are several salon furniture styles and the electrical needs for each.

- **Wall hanging station with no bottom cabinet**

  This style station is widely used with an outlet which is usually located underneath. The blower and curling iron are located on the right of the station.

- **Wall station to the floor**

  The outlet is located, in most cases, on the right side of the station.

- **Continuous station on the wall**

  The design has all the wall-style units connected and the electric needs to be mounted on the face of the cabinet. The electric comes from the wall with flexible BX (electrical) cable that is connected to the outlet located on the station.

- **Freestanding back-to-back styling station**

  The unit needs electric either coming from the floor or the ceiling. Unless electric from the floor is already in place, you will have to cut the floor to get electric to it. Some owners just run a strip plug to the unit and keep the station a few feet from the wall. This is unsightly and presents a trip hazard, but it is an inexpensive option. The other alternative is to have the electric come from the ceiling, which usually has acoustical tile. The electric is covered with either hard conduit line or flexible BX cable. Most clients cover the line cosmetically.

Below find typical recommendations. Many cities and states have different construction requirements.

Wall station to the floor

Wall station with leg support

Freestanding back-to-back styling station

Permits—Electric

If permits are needed, here is the process (Friday evening – reopen Tuesday morning). We recommend you close on Saturday because of the unusual amount of electrical work and coordination for this process.

1. On Friday, call for inspection for Monday afternoon.

2. If possible, deliver all furniture that requires electrical work for inspection on Friday. If there is no room in the salon for this, have it delivered on Saturday.

3. Friday evening, demolish all old cabinets and equipment/furniture concerning electric.

4. Start installing equipment/furniture Saturday and finish either that day or Sunday.

5. Electrician comes in Saturday afternoon to start working and to make sure he has the right supplies to handle the job.

6. Electrician works on all new connections, moving whatever electrical is needed and reconnects all outlets.

7. Work is finished by noon Monday and inspector approves and signs off on permits.

8. Open on Tuesday.

Permits—Drywall

The work may get done after hours when the salon is closed or during a few hours every evening. It all depends on how extensive the work is. Two things you must be aware of concerning permits when working on partitions or building rooms:

1. The room or partition can only be built on one side and cannot be closed until you have approval from the framing inspector.

2. If there is any electrical or plumbing going in the wall, you will need a "rough" inspection before you close up the other side.

Once these inspections are approved, you can close up the wall and finish the room or partition. This just needs to be coordinated. You might be able to handle all of this while you are open—it all depends on the scope of the work. Discuss this with your contractor to strategize the best approach.

A Transformation Weekend

Many salon owners decide not to pull permits for the work they are doing. A lot of the work may be cosmetic and the subcontractors they use are licensed, but the salon owner may get talked out of plans and permits because of the delay. Ready, Set, Go! recommends "pulling permits," but if you decide not to, please use a licensed subcontractor, not a handyman with talent. Below, is a step-by-step process on how to handle this transformation so you can reopen as soon as possible.

Before You Get Started

Hopefully, you decided to consult a professional in the industry to help guide you with the equipment/furniture you purchased. Many salon design companies give you a space-plan, drawings, and specifications on everything you purchased. Just before the work begins, we recommend a group meeting with all the subcontractors and your designer. Have all of the drawings and specifications on hand for all to review and ask questions. Coordinate a schedule so everyone is on the same path and understands the schedule completely. Hopefully, the furniture is at the location and everyone can see exactly what is involved.

Your old furniture must be considered in the transformation process for removal or it might have some value. Here are some recommended selling prices for your used equipment and furniture:

- Styling chairs: $25 to $50 depending on make, model, and condition.
- Dryer chair: $35 to $50.
- Reception desk: small (4 to 5 feet), $50 to $100; large desk, $100 to $500.
- Shampoo sinks: $25; if they are marble or porcelain style, $50 to $75.
- Shampoo chairs: $25.
- Freestanding sink units: $50 to $100. If they are European or were expensive when new, $100 to $300.
- Styling stations: simple stations, $10 to $25. Freestanding or custom units, $50 to $200.
- Nail tables: $25 to $50.
- Nail stools: $10.
- Pedicure unit: $50 to $100 for base model; for motorized unit, $250 to $500.
- Facial tables: standard style, $25 to $75; for a hydraulic or electric style, $100 to $500.
- Skin care unit: $100 to $300.
- Reception chairs: $10 to $50.
- Retail units: $25 to $300.
- Mirrors: $10 to $25.
- Dispensary cabinets: anything!

> **NOTE**
> Advertise old furniture on Craigslist in your local area to sell it. Get rid of it at any price. If not, it will cost you to move it.

These prices can vary widely. Remember, you are giving these people good prices as long as they are willing to pick up the equipment or furniture on your schedule and timeline. If you don't trade it in or sell it, you need to haul it away and that will cost hundreds of dollars.

Preparation

Put up a sign well in advance to let your clients know when you are remodeling; be sure to include closed and reopen dates on the sign. It is also good to show the new design and some of the new equipment and furniture on a presentation board; this will excite the clients and staff. Several of your staff will give their opinion on the furniture, including their likes and dislikes. Be diplomatic, but remember, this is your business and it's what YOU want to do. Book your last appointment early Saturday afternoon and have your staff ready.

The Start

1. Have boxes for each staff member to clean out their station. Have them bring the box home or store it somewhere on the premises out of the way.

2. Have the front desk team do the same process and clean out the front desk. Also, mark the boxes for all your retail and try to keep it organized for restocking the shelves.

3. Bring your computer person in to unhook and pack your credit card processor and computer system so they can reinstall it when ready and not misplace any cables or wires.

Now the Real Fun Begins

1. Tear out all unwanted furniture, cabinets, chairs, pedicure units—whatever you are remodeling—and have your salon equipment/furniture company or "buyers" pick it up. Try to clear the space as much as possible so your installers or contractors are not tripping over each other.

2. For the tear-out, your electrician and plumber will need to be there to unhook the existing sinks and any existing electrical that may be attached to the old cabinets.

3. Your plumber and electrician will start modifying plumbing or electrical for the new equipment/furniture.

4. At the same time, bring in all of the new equipment/furniture for installation. Try to work in places that are not in the way of the plumber or electrician.

5. Coordinate with the subcontractors on hooking everything up.

6. Once everything is installed, call your staff to set up their stations or department.

7. Call your computer person to hook up your system and credit card terminal.

8. As everything is being set up, you can do any light assembly work, such as building the styling chairs or dryer chairs. These items are very simple to put together.

9. Set up your retail, clean the salon, and get ready to open in the morning.

What we described can be done in a four-day period, closing late Saturday afternoon, and opening up on Thursday for business. All you need is good coordination and good subcontractors who are committed to getting your project done and your salon reopened in a timely manner.

We recently remodeled Jon Lori Salon in Fair Haven, New Jersey. The salon owner had the commitment described above and did a complete face-lift over a four-day period. The installation crew worked until 2:00 a.m. the day they reopened. A cleaning crew came in at 3:00 a.m. and they were finished and ready to reopen by 9:00 a.m. The secret was hard work and dedication from everyone involved.

Things to remember when starting your remodeling project:

○ Let customers know about what's going on and what to expect.

○ If you have a plan for a new design and layout, frame and display it for all to see.

○ Plan for delays. Murphy's Law may or may not strike your salon remodel project, but anticipate delays.

○ If money is needed from your banker, work out all details before you think about starting your remodel project.

○ Box all things that may be in the way of contractors and furniture/equipment installers.

○ Plan all of your clients' appointments around work schedules.

○ Plan that major construction or your new equipment install during the evening or when you are closed over the weekend.

Salon Owner/Operators Discuss the Good, the Bad, & the Ugly

Sue Gahr, Owner of Studio 2 Hair Salon, Point Pleasant, NJ

"The best part of remodeling the salon I bought from my former employer was now having the ability to add what I felt would make the salon "me!" I wanted my customers to feel welcome and comfortable. I wanted a salon that I could call home and be proud of. When I was finished with my remodel, that's exactly how it was. My customers are happy and so am I. The worst part was realizing I had to get rid of nails. I needed the room for my hair business. The person I had to let go was a friend and colleague. I know a lot about hair and color, that is my passion. I knew nothing about nails. I had to let it go."

Liz Howell, Get It Together Hair and Nail Salon, Houston, TX

"The worst thing I did was not have a budget. What started as a small remodel turned into a three-month project. My budget was blown, and because I didn't plan well, it cost me a fortune with my contractor. Plan, budget, and put a timeline together. Without that, don't do it. Plus, I had no idea custom equipment could take as long as 10 to 12 weeks to get made. That killed me."

CHAPTER 41

Surviving the First Year—What to Expect & How to Adjust

The first year of owning your salon is the most important. It sets the stage and determines whether you are set up for success or failure. Opening a new business and surviving the first year will be the hardest thing you do in your life.

Businesses that open their doors and are instant hits are a rare commodity. If that were the case, everyone would do it. Many small businesses expect this to happen to their business and this scenario is unrealistic.

The sad fact is that the vast majority of businesses fail within the first year. It is especially true for business owners who don't have the experience they need to adjust to the challenges of daily business, employees, payroll and taxes, plus everything else that comes along with running a successful salon. Have you ever heard the following sayings about making it through the first year?

- *"If you break even the first year, you are doing well."*
- *"If you survived the first year, you are on your way to becoming a successful business owner."*

Both of these sayings are so true. Follow these strategies to stay ahead of the game and avoid the common pitfalls and troubles that most salon owners face during the first year—whether it's your first salon or your second or third salon. Zeroing in on these tactics will help bring your business back in line and help you to be more profitable.

Stay on Budget

During the first year of business, entrepreneurs spend most of their startup money. Success doesn't happen overnight. Try to avoid making unnecessary purchases. Stick with the bare minimum of what you need. Increase inventory as your business grows; don't go out and buy a year's worth of products upfront. Increase business items as your business grows.

There will be many bills to pay, and not enough profit to compensate for them—at least not yet. You will need to watch every nickel you make. Keeping accurate financial records is a must. One of the most common problems an entrepreneur faces during the first year is falling behind on payroll taxes for business income. Once you fall behind on your taxes, it is difficult to get back on track.

Your business will need to budget for taxes and your profits need to be high enough to pay those taxes and still yield cash to cover other expenses. The last person on the list to be paid most of the time will be you! Remember, "Rome wasn't built in a day." Building a business takes time.

Product Supply Credit

To be successful, you must align yourself with a manufacturer or product distributor who will give you a business line of credit. You can then buy retail products and pay monthly instead of all at once. Doing this will enable you to budget your retail products as a monthly expense. Buy only what you need and do not go overboard. You also want to form an alliance with your distributor for exclusivity in your area or community. Competition is healthy, but not if someone else in your area is selling the same products.

This alliance will enable you to sell your products at a much higher margin, allowing more profits in the initial stages of your business.

Adjust

Too many startups fail because their owners simply don't acknowledge what's going wrong. It is important for you to be honest with yourself about how your business is faring and adjust accordingly. If there are aspects of your salon that seemed like a good idea, but aren't bringing in revenue, get rid of them. Don't continue to throw good, hard-earned money at something that is not working. If something in your business model needs tweaking, don't wait too long. Tackle it before it is too late.

Learning During the First Year & Beyond

The first year is your learning curve, enabling you to better understand your market, get to know your clients, and find good employees. It will take time to become familiar with your retail products. Getting to know your products better than anyone else takes valuable time. Getting to know your staff and blending the personalities in the salon is not something that happens overnight.

It is also important to get to know your target market and your clients. It is possible that you need improvements in these areas. Being your own boss allows you to look at these problems and make changes instantly.

Adjusting to change is a good thing. Think out of the box and you will adapt. Listen to employees, friends and family, and your clients when it comes to business ideas and solving problems you have. Have a suggestion box on the desk as you enter the salon. Be open to suggestions, no matter how minute or ridiculous they may seem.

Remember, if you are always talking, you can't be listening. Without listening, you are not learning. Become a good listener!

Remember, you need to keep up on the latest trends for your industry and learn about salon management and small business success strategies. Experienced salon owners know just how much learning occurs during the first year, but they'll be the first to tell you that it doesn't really stop. There is always something more to learn and ways to push yourself to be a better manager, service provider, and business owner.

Focus on Your Core Business

Identify all the business elements you need in order for your business to grow and set everything else aside for now. If you decide to focus on color in your salon, then do that. Focus on hair color and advertise your salon as the best in your area for this work. Educate your staff in hair color. Have your distributor bring in marketing materials, such as graphics, for your windows and samples.

The biggest mistake in the first year is trying to promise and deliver everything to your clients. It's better to under promise and over deliver. Sure, you may have big ideas for how you want to grow your business and how you eventually want to diversify, but it is important to get on solid ground before you start challenging yourself and your staff to do new things. Walk before you run. Growing your business slowly is not a bad thing. It will enable you to better manage your time, family life, finances, staff, and your clients.

NOTE

Being a jack-of-all-trades and master of none is not a good practice in the salon marketplace.

CHAPTER 42

Successful Retail

"The road to success is always under construction."
—W. Clement Stone

Salons that want success in retail need to make sure they do the tasks that will result in a good income from retail sales. It is particularly true in these tough economic times when many businesses are struggling to stay afloat. We have gone over many of the reasons why you may fail, like opening in the wrong location, not having enough capital, or dealing with personnel issues.

These may be factors that could drag your retail business down. However, the true question of whether your salon will do well has less to do with all those factors and more to do with you.

You are a salon owner! The reason you opened a salon was to build a successful business—and to make money! Don't forget you are also very talented in your profession and on the cutting-edge of style. Your salon and staff needs to portray the importance of fashion and style for your clients. The retail products your salon carries should set the retail and fashion trends in the industry today. Product manufacturers understand the fashion trend of the moment. To achieve your retailing goals, you should let your clients know that you keep current and that you carry only the newest, best products.

Clients are looking for value; it is an important factor in today's world. We did say "value," not "price." Your salon needs to offer an assortment of retail, not just one brand. If you do go with the one-brand strategy, you must carry the full product line, giving your customer the ability to purchase something that fits in their price range.

When you focus on value, it will enable you to sell more merchandise. This will open up the door for your manufacturer to provide you with better pricing. Doing so should enable you to pass these savings on to your clients. Furthermore, manufacturers will come to you first with promotions and education and new product lines. You will continue to be on top of the trends before your competitors.

Creating Retail Awareness

The basic premise of a retailing business is simple, right? You buy products from a distributor or manufacturer at wholesale and sell it for more than you paid for it. Unfortunately, the things in life that seem like they should be simple are often the most difficult to master. Several variables come into play when selling retail in your salon.

Manufacturers who specialize in salon retail products have identified the following most common retailing mistakes:

- **Overpricing:** If clients feel they can get a lower price somewhere else, they will shop there instead of at your salon.

- **Not understanding the products you sell:** If your salon sales team does not understand what your products are used for and how they benefit the services you offer, then you will not be successful in selling retail.

- **Not knowing what your competitors sell and how they do it:** If your salon sells the same products as a competitor, why should your clients buy from you instead of the other salon down the street? Visit the salon as a client to understand what they do, how they price their products, and what makes your salon different. Ignoring a good competitor in your marketplace means you are letting them take business away from you.

- **Having no plan to sell:** You need to plan exactly how you will sell your products. The plan should include advertising, signage, sales team and front desk training, and special salon promotions.

- **Buying too much product:** Retailing is expensive. Having excessive inventory sitting in boxes does not make you money. Most salon owners are optimistic by nature, but you should never buy your retailing products based on optimism.

- **Buying from too many vendors:** Putting your eggs in one retail basket is not a good idea, but so is spreading yourself too thin with multiple vendors. You will never have strong enough buying power when offering multiple product lines. You will probably not have the ability to properly educate your team on selling multiple brands. Having too many brands also confuses your customers.

- **Selling items that your clients can't afford:** We all want to sell and be associated with high-end, beautiful products. The problem that we run into with salon retailing is understanding what your clients can afford. It's simple; if you have retail that is priced beyond what your client is willing to pay, they will not be able to shop at your salon for products.

- **Poor display or hidden items:** Every item that you sell should have at least one moment in the sun during the day. Your clients have to see it to buy it. If it's buried and out of the spotlight, then it's not going to sell. Out of sight, out of mind!

- **Competition:** Do you think you have to lower your price to meet or beat what the competition is doing? No, you don't. Remember, your salon should be better-educated, have better pricing with your manufacturer/distributors, offer perfect customer service, and understand your clients' needs.

- **Markdowns:** When an item doesn't sell, it is time to mark down the product to try to move the item. Trying to sell something that is not moving, leads to feelings of frustration and results in zero sales. If it doesn't sell, mark it down. Get rid of it and stop ordering that product.

- **Not knowing your current promotions, specials, and pricing:** Your salon team should be savvy when it comes to selling retail. If they do not know the salon's current promotions, specials, and pricing, how are they going to sell retail to their customers? Educate your team weekly on any specials your salon is running. It is imperative to successful retailing.

Motivating Your Sales Team Doesn't Always Take Money!

What motivates your employees? You can have the most beautiful salon in the greatest neighborhood with a constant flow of business, but that doesn't guarantee that your staff is happy.

You must figure out a true win-win for you and your salon team so they feel they are being rewarded properly for their contribution to retail sales. Once this is done, you will be on a fast track to retail success.

Below, you will find other benefits and ideas, besides money, that you can offer your staff to motivate and reward their sales performance.

Employee discounts: As you can imagine, knowledge of the retail you sell is key. You should encourage your salon employees to use the products they sell. Offer only a certain amount of product for personal use each month, but let them purchase it at cost. Using the products at home will give them firsthand experience with the products. They will be able to provide their own testimony about the products and why they love them, which helps your employees to be more genuine with your clients when they are representing your salon and the products you carry. As an extra incentive, you should also give them a "friends and family" discount on retail items.

Learning and earning: When you completely understand what you are selling, you have more power behind your message and your retail offer. Education is a must! Give your salon staff the opportunity each week to learn about the retail business, not just the products. Product manufacturers offer education—take full advantage of this as much as possible. Devoting a few hours a week to product education will reward you many times over with continued retail success.

Make it fun: The daily grind of trying to manage work and family has most of us on edge. Working in a salon environment is not easy. Most salon employees stand on their feet for more than eight hours in any given day and they are client-facing, meaning they are on stage when they are on the floor. Given the physical demands and customer service requirement of their work, it's important to provide a fun environment. We are not talking about having late-night parties or trips to the bar. We are talking about contests and keeping your staff motivated. For example, set a goal and reward the top achiever with a dinner out on the town or a special gift for the top retailer of the month or quarter.

We all deserve a title: We all reach a point in life where we want to be recognized. The job title we have or the significance of the level of education we have earned is important to how we feel about ourselves. A simple business card with the title and name is a good start. Having these business cards printed for your entire staff is a very inexpensive way to make your salon a special place to work. Each of your employees should have this, no matter what their role.

We all need some time: Many salons are open seven days a week and some are open for a full 12 hours on most days. The extended hours of a salon and a good retail store must meet the needs of the clients. Salon owners need to remember that staff may need flexibility to run an errand or take a day off for family. When this arises, be flexible. Work out scheduling with your staff around work and family. Being flexible with one of your top employees may enable you to keep a strong retail salesperson. Be careful and fair about your policies for taking time off.

Work environment: We have all been touched by the latest recession. We have watched the business world melt down and the headlines shouting war and terrorism for over ten years. Many of us have changed the way we go about our daily lives. We look differently for things to make us happy other than spending money on materialistic things. Many of us find enjoyment at work. The salon environment has always been a social place to meet and greet new and loyal clients while providing a service to make them look and feel good about themselves. Your salon should be the anchor in your community. Your staff should always feel that they are something much more than an employee in your salon. This will ultimately give them the enthusiasm to come to work and feel good about being there to serve your salon's clients. It's up to you to build this type of salon environment.

Selling Retail Is Not That Difficult

Your clients come to you and stay with you because they trust you. You give them an environment where they can escape the everyday nuisances of work and family. This downtime is usually one of the best times of their day. They come to you not only for their haircut or color, but also to socialize and chat about all that is going on in their lives.

You, as their hairdresser, have to understand and listen to what their needs are. You should know what hair products they use and what you sold them the last time they were in the salon for service.

While concentrating on the service you are providing to your client, you should also think about what retail products you will suggest for them. While working on your client, chat about what they need in regard to hair products and make suggestions. Listen to what they say and look for opportunities to match what they are telling you with the products that can help them. For example, do they have concerns about frizzy hair, thinning hair, or color-treated hair? Do they swim or spend a lot of time in the sun? All of these are good conversation starters and can help you to suggest the right product that will solve their hair challenge.

When they have finished talking, take the time to make thoughtful suggestions. Suggestive selling is a very easy way to mention promotions, along with products that you think will help them look the best with the service you just completed. I find that this type of selling completes the service and experience you are offering. You give the feeling that you are confident and educated in the products you use and sell in the salon.

The concept of suggestive selling is simple. When a client comes into the salon for a service or to buy haircare products, you have an opportunity to discover the complementary products that would be best suited to that person and their needs. For example, if you are selling shampoo to a client, there is a good possibility he or she may need conditioner or hairspray to go along with it.

Suggesting the conditioner is not being pushy. This is something most salon owners don't understand—the customer is already in your salon for service, why let them buy their haircare products at the grocery store? They don't go to the grocery store to get their haircut or to have their hair colored! This should be used as a major advantage that an owner-operator uses when selling retail. Salon products are made to be sold in a salon environment.

To avoid any element of pushy selling in your salon, follow these suggestions:

- Recommend the most logical of all the additional items that could complete the client's original purchase.
- Look at what they purchased the last time they were in for service, check to see how they liked it, and ask if their supply is still good.
- If their supply of the last product is still good, ask about a complementary product that is in the same line.
- Introduce the client to a brand new product by letting them take home a sample.
- If the client says no, stop right there.

Suggestive selling is one of the most important parts of providing your client with a complete salon experience and powerful customer service. How will your client know that you have products to extend their color or look unless you tell them? Like becoming a master stylist or colorist, suggestive selling will take a certain amount of time and practice to master. Once your salon team gets this down, it will be great for your staff, clients, and business.

Ability to Work With People Is a Must

It is important that you have open communication with people so that you can run a successful retail environment. Understand your clients and teach your staff how to understand them too so that you approach your clients in the same friendly, educational, and supportive way. An aggressive sales approach may work in some businesses. But, in a salon, a more delicate approach is needed.

Your employees are the key to your success. They must know your products in and out. They must follow your business code as discussed in Chapter 30. The code will give them an idea of exactly how you want them to approach your clients. If you and your staff learn to get along with everyone and build relationships with your clients, they will trust you when making a product recommendation. If your clients feel like they are safe and in a warm, trusting environment, they will be dedicated to you and the retail you are selling every time they come for a service or salon visit.

Ambition, Drive, & Self-Motivation

These three qualities go hand-in-hand to make you the kind of person who can keep a salon retail environment thriving no matter what is going on with the economy. You must have ambitious goals for your salon and the drive to work hard to achieve these goals. You need to have the knack to sell yourself, your products, and your system. You have to believe passionately in what you are selling. People who are lazy, prefer to be told what to do, or lack internal drive, will not do well in the retail business.

Thirst for Knowledge

To be successful in retail, you need to stay on top of all of the information you receive on the products you are selling. The knowledge has to trickle down to your staff. It will manifest itself most if you have a passion for the beauty industry. To be a success, you must have that passion and share it. The thirst for knowledge will encourage you to learn and gain the confidence needed to successfully sell retail products to your clients.

Five tips for creating a better understanding of products:

- Distributor education on products
- Trade shows
- Weekly staff meetings on retail sales
- Live demonstrations on new products
- Workshops

Leadership

Owning the salon doesn't make you a leader; it only makes you the person in charge. Being a leader requires you to be innovative, a good listener, and open to new ideas, a visionary. With your willingness to experiment, you will make the salon more effective. You also have to have a forgiving heart and realize that sometimes people aren't making mistakes on purpose—they just don't know. You also have to be willing to change when what you are doing is not working.

A leader must have integrity. As a leader, you are vulnerable, just like everyone else. You must always maintain an upbeat attitude about life and business. People want to be around positive people with high energy. There will be many ups and downs in the retail business. Your staff will look to you to guide them through this.

An optimistic attitude will let you find creative solutions to the daily and ongoing problems that may arise in your business.

Retail management tips you should practice in your salon.

○ Train for the cause.

○ Lead by example.

○ Motivate your staff.

○ Coach continuously.

○ Communicate to your employees and customers.

○ Be honest and have integrity.

○ Manage performance.

○ Mentor and develop people.

○ Praise and reward team members for successful retail sales.

○ Manage up.

○ Educate on your products weekly.

○ Take action.

○ Develop a flair for visual merchandising.

○ Work hard for results.

○ Be enthusiastic, ambitious, and energetic about retail.

○ Learn as much as you can.

○ Be a leader.

Christy Phan

"Be very careful on selecting what product line to bring in for retail and who you want to select to be part of your team! Go with your deepest instinct and don't worry about what your stylists say because they always want more and more, and that usually brought a lot of negatives and stress. Breathe and take it easy!"

Rome Anna R. Saldivar

"Expanded retail product selection to include a "stylists' favorites" shelf so they can use and recommend their favorite and/or new products to clients and each other."

Dermal-Care Esthetics

"Expanded retail product, and hired independent contractors (massage therapists, acupuncturist, etc.)."

Julianna's Main Street Hair, Staten Island, NY

"I educate my staff weekly on the products we sell. I have weekly and monthly retail sales contests. The winner gets a dinner out on me at their favorite restaurant. They love the competition. It works. Also, they know they earn more when they sell products."

CHAPTER 43

Keep It Clean

"When making a fire, people like to join you; when cleaning the ashes, you are often alone."

—Chinese Proverb

One of the most important concerns in a salon should be that it is clean and clutter-free. Clients will not want to frequent a salon that does not seem to care about cleanliness. If your clients are aware of the high standards you set for cleanliness, it reassures their confidence in you and your establishment.

While nobody wants to take out the trash, clean a bathroom, or sweep the floor around their workstation, every business needs someone to do these things. You may designate one of your employees to do these daily chores or hire a commercial cleaning service.

- Sweeping, dusting, and making sure the bathroom is spotless should be on the daily "To Do" list.

- Clean Workstations should be cleaned thoroughly after each client, which is necessary for sanitary reasons and cleanliness. If you cut someone's hair, the worst thing you can do is bring a client over to your station and have them walk through someone else's hair. It is also a hazard. A client could lose their footing and easily slip and fall on a hair-filled floor.

- Different services and treatments require different sanitary measures. Let your clients know you cleaned the tools being used before the service.

- Foot spas should be cleaned thoroughly and rinsed after each use.

- The manicuring area also must be sterilized after each use. Sanitizing the tools used for manicures or pedicures protects the client and your manicurist from disease.

- When applying makeup and creams, make sure you wipe the entire area after each client to prevent cross-contamination. Lotions, makeup products, and wax pots are susceptible to bacteria. These locations should be cleaned immediately after each use.

- Make sure garbage pails are empty. Clients do not like looking at other people's trash. Empty them two to three times in the course of a day.

- Check the bathrooms every hour. You do not want a dirty bathroom in your beauty salon. Make sure the garbage pail is empty at all times. Consumables must be restocked.

- All combs, brushes, and clips should be sanitized after each use.

- Retail shelving and products must be dusted daily. Dust on retail means it isn't selling. That will surely result in poor retailing in your salon. Keep this area spotless.

- Clutter is a big mistake in the salon. The image you want in your salon is not one where stations are covered with notes and pictures and social obligations. Your workspace should be clear of clutter. There should be a place for everything and everything in its place.

- Take a good look at your employees. Are his/her nails kept neat and tidy? A hairstylist who looks like they need a bath should not be working in your salon. Their hair, nails, and makeup are an image of your salon and business.

- Sanitizers should be placed in multiple locations for your staff and clients.

Cleanliness is next to profitability. This should be an important part of your salon culture. Your staff should take pride in keeping the salon clean. It's up to you, as the owner, to set the guidelines when it comes to employees keeping their workspace spotless.

Set a schedule and explain the what, when, who, and how of the duties expected from each of your employees. If you put simple systems in place, everyone can tell normal from abnormal at a glance. You can also post pictures of what a clean area looks like to demonstrate what is expected.

If you set the expectations and support the behavior, this aspect of running your salon will practically run itself.

Commercial Cleaning Service

If cleaning the salon becomes too much of a burden as your business grows, there are commercial cleaning companies that will assist in the daily, weekly, and monthly cleaning of your salon.

Best of all, reputable cleaning services are fully licensed and insured, which protects your business property from theft and damage.

Commercial cleaning services deliver an array of services. The most common day-to-day janitorial services you should expect will include:

- Disposing of the salon's trash
- Sweeping, vacuuming, mopping, and waxing the floors in the common area
- Washing interior windows
- Cleaning the bathrooms, sinks, and stalls (replenish consumables)
- Dusting and cleaning retail shelving and workstations (keep in mind they will not move personal property)
- Wiping down all salon equipment
- Dusting ceiling and light fixtures

In addition to the basic day-to-day cleaning, you can discuss items that you may need cleaned once a month or as a deep cleaning when necessary. Commercial cleaning services may also take care of picking up trash in your parking lot or maintain heating and air conditioning equipment.

Hiring the right cleaning company should be easy. You can use a large, national company, or you may have more luck with a local, community-based company. Smaller companies may be more flexible and able to work within your budget as your business is growing. Check with your landlord or other tenants for a cleaning company. They may be able to recommend a reliable company.

Most cleaning companies base their price on square footage of your space and how many bathrooms they have to clean. If you have a large dispensary or color lab with a sink, they may charge you more because of these spaces.

> **NOTE**
>
> Cleaning your business is something you must do so well that nobody notices—until you don't do it!

Commercial cleaning companies usually bring their own cleaning supplies and equipment. They will come and clean after hours so as not to disrupt your business.

When you decided to go into business, many of these chores probably fell on you, the owner of the business. You were probably the janitor until you were able to afford the staff or cleaning service to take the burden.

CHAPTER 44

Going Green

"You must be the change you wish to see in the world."
—Mahatma Gandhi

For almost half a century, environmentalists have advocated that big businesses incorporate sustainability principles into their practices. Yet even ten years ago, it was rare to hear of any business with dedicated "green" or environmental practices. Today, green is mainstream, and it is big business. A recent study found clean-energy technology outpaced all other sectors in job growth and investments, even in a recession.

In the U.S., we currently face two historic sets of challenges, one to our economy and the other to our environment. At the same time, people here and across the world are facing immediate and impending impacts of climate change, such as disastrous droughts, melting arctic ice, and destructive storms.

The emerging clean-energy economy can solve both sets of problems. It has the potential to drive innovation and stimulate a sustainable economic recovery that changes the environmentally harmful "business as usual" practices of the past. Where other people might see problems and crises, innovative green business leaders see opportunity. Waves of companies, both large and small, are using success in business to achieve social and environmental change. These emerging business models seek to preserve environmental quality, promote social equality, and stimulate sustainable economic growth.

Despite the business potential of such green innovation, many entrepreneurs still feel that they do not have the capital or the know-how needed to operate a green business. These suggestions can help boost sales, reduce operating costs, increase returns for investors, and establish you as an environmental business leader in your community.

By integrating green initiatives into your operations, you can help conserve natural resources and reduce your contribution to global warming. Going green in your salon is not an expensive investment. You can start with your cleaning chemicals and go from there. Going green can impact the bottom line in these ways:

• Increase Net Earnings

Going green has the potential to increase net earnings by both driving increased revenues and reducing operating expenses. Developing environmentally sustainable products and services can spur new sales to end users and large retailers in a growing consumer sector, which can increase top line revenues.

• Appeal to a Consumer Demand

Whether selling directly to consumers or to other businesses, the market demand is high for green products and services and environmentally conscious companies.

• Increase Chances of Receiving Critical Financing

With the passage of the American Recovery and Reinvestment Act (ARRA) and many state initiatives, a number of financial resources are available for companies that are creating jobs and contributing to the green economy. In addition, private-sector investment opportunities for green enterprises are growing.

Here are ten tips to green your business, reduce your impact on the environment, and save money:

1. Educate yourself and your staff on what it means to go green.
2. Create a lead or point person to help create the "green team."
3. Talk to your staff about not only what can be done in the salon, but also in your homes or other frequented places.
4. Conserve energy.
5. Conserve water.
6. Reduce paper waste.
7. Use better environmental products.
8. Reduce any toxins used in your workplace.
9. Become green consumers.
10. Obtain green product certification.

Overall, be aware of helping the environment, promote it, and market your business as an organization that is "green friendly." Your customers will like the fact that your salon is going green. Promote your green products in or around the salon. Have green bathroom products. It's not just a trend; it is part of keeping our planet a better place for future generations. If you cannot measure what it is doing for your business, you can measure what it is doing for the environment!

CHAPTER 45

Energy-Saving Tips

When You Save Energy, You Save Money

When starting your business, you will be overrun with many different tasks that you haven't done in the past. Your job description will be a mile long—handling payroll, scheduling your staff, running to the bank, making merchant payments and charges, and juggling your family. The thing that bothers all of us as business owners is opening the mail and seeing exactly what it costs each month to run and operate the salon. The dreaded bills come in every month no matter what. There are fixed expenses that we can't change like rent, payroll, insurances, and product expenses. Isn't it nice to know you can control and improve something with little effort? That's right, it's saving energy! When you save energy, you save money.

Tips to Save Energy

The biggest part of your energy bill at the salon will be heating and air conditioning. You want your clients to be comfortable when visiting and getting services at the salon. However, you can reduce these costs without making your clients aware that you are on a cost-saving mission.

For instance, turn down the heat or air conditioning when no one is in the salon, preferably at night and on Sundays and Mondays if the salon is closed. Install new electronic timers that will automatically shut the system down or set the thermostat at an adequate level for an empty salon. Set the thermostat to a comfortable setting two hours prior to your salon opening. The most important maintenance task that will also ensure efficiency of your heat and air conditioning unit is to replace or clean the filters monthly. Clogged, dirty filters affect normal airflow and significantly reduce a system's efficiency. Thus, when the filters are dirty, the system is working harder and using more energy, which increases your bill.

Installing ceiling fans gives your salon a comfortable look, but it will also have a major effect on cost savings during the summer and winter months. The fans will circulate the air, which can make the salon five degrees cooler during the summer months, reducing the time your air conditioning system is running. Most fans have two settings. The "forward" or "clockwise" setting is used during the winter months to push warm trapped air down and pull cooler air upwards. The "counter-clockwise" setting produces a comfortable breeze that will keep your clients cool during the summer months. Remember, you will need to switch the direction of your fan when the seasons change.

Appliances

The key to saving energy is buying energy-efficient appliances. The appliances should be Energy Star labeled products. If purchasing a refrigerator for your salon break room, or a washer and dryer for your towels and capes, spend the few dollars more for an energy-efficient machine. It may cost more when you make the purchase, but it will save you up to 4 percent a month on your electric bill.

Washer

When using your washer, make sure it is full. Do not wash towels on the hot setting. Use the cool setting; this also will save you money. It only works if you let your staff know how you want things done. Put directions right on the washer. They will get the point.

Dryer

Drying your salon's towels and capes is essential; it is also one of the primary sources of wasted energy. Install a dryer vent seal to save energy. This will eliminate any drafts from entering the salon when the dryer is not in use and could easily reduce the salon's heating costs.

Don't overload the dryer. Overloading the dryer means it takes as much as three times longer to dry. You must have room in the dryer for items to tumble. Towels will never dry if there is no room to tumble. It will also reduce the life of the dryer. That could result in a heavy repair bill or replacement.

Lighting

Lighting is not only necessary, but is decorative, especially in the salon environment. We have become accustomed to placing light wherever we desire. Light is essential when trying to capture hair color or allowing a client to see the new style you have created for them. There are still ways to cut back and reduce electric costs. Replace as many incandescent light bulbs (the standard bulbs that get very hot), with energy-efficient CFLs (compact fluorescent lights). These bulbs use as much as two-thirds less energy than standard light bulbs and last twice as long. You can save $30 or more in energy costs over the lifetime of each bulb.

If you have lighting in your parking lot or on the side of your building, reduce the lighting by using solar-powered path lighting or place the unit on a timer.

Computers

There is no need to have computers running 24-hours a day in the salon; that's wasting energy and costing you money. You should preset your computer so that it either shuts down or hibernates when it's not in use. You can install an energy-saving smart strip to your salon's computer and support devices. The smart strip device senses when you have shut down your computer and then shuts down all the devices automatically.

Team Effort

Saving energy is part of a salon team approach. Shutting down bathroom lights when not in use, not overloading the dryer, and turning down the thermostat is something everyone in your salon has to have the discipline to do. We suggest you have a staff meeting about energy-saving ideas and guidelines so that everyone is on the same page. Remember, when you save energy, you are saving money!

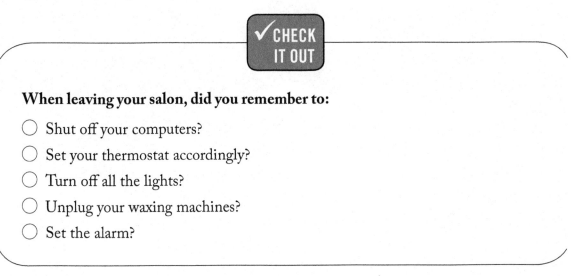

When leaving your salon, did you remember to:

○ Shut off your computers?

○ Set your thermostat accordingly?

○ Turn off all the lights?

○ Unplug your waxing machines?

○ Set the alarm?

Wellness Spa at the Pfister Hotel- Milwaukee, WI

CHAPTER 46

Design Professionals Discuss Startup Mistakes

Written by Sales Professionals, Takara Belmont.

When it comes to designing a salon, you may feel you certainly have the creativity. Let's face it—you have awareness of style, fashion, and beauty. That is why you chose cosmetology in the first place, right? But, designing your salon without professional help can lead to many mistakes in functionality, space-planning, and business operations.

To give you additional insights, we talked with industry leaders in salon design and layout about some of the top three mistakes that salons have made and how to correct them.

1. Eclectic Salon (Jeff Holmes – Takara Belmont, Regional Sales Manager)

"We are always put back by the design term 'eclectic' as it relates to salon environments. Generally, this means the owner wants to access salon furniture from a number of different sources and from home furnishing stores. These furnishings are not intended for use in the salon. The result is a confusing design and a salon in which it can be difficult to conduct business. The salon owners also think they can attract higher-end clientele and charge higher prices for their services without investing in high quality salon furnishings."

2. Never Enough Time (Carolyn Collins – Takara Belmont, Regional Sales Manager, NE)

"Time frame is always a common problem when it comes to building a salon. People don't understand the process it takes to put together a beautiful, functional salon. Customers never seem to leave enough time to file the proper building permits they need when doing this type of project. You should always allow four to six weeks for permit time. In some cities, it takes longer. It becomes the designer's problem because they expect us to get things done quicker when they didn't allow enough time with the landlord for the building process. Usually, you will need 90 to 120 days from the time the permits are filed. Always push the landlord for as much free rent time as possible. The thing we hear the most is, 'Can I open in 30 days?' That's highly unlikely."

3. Knowing All the Costs (Michael Caron – Takara Belmont, Regional Manager West)

"The project location was in San Francisco, fourth floor of a building built in the 1940s (this was key). The two partners were not hairstylists, had loads of money, but no clue of the industry. Did all the right things—hired a local architect; the contractor visited all the equipment companies' showrooms. It was to be a full-service salon with 28 stations, a manicure/pedicure, a full, four-room spa area. The design and concept was stellar. The overall budget was $750K with an equipment purchase at about $135K. Everything was telling me this was to be an outstanding project."

Here is what went down:

- *The initial concept for the aesthetic statement of the outside walls of the spa area was to have silk-screened glass panels, approximately 12. Production started on them and then stopped when it was discovered that the cost to insure and 'crane' them up to the fourth floor was more than the panels themselves. The [installation] occurred four weeks prior to the opening date. A totally different approach was needed. $$$*

- *Pedicure unit specification sheet was not provided to the contractor's plumbing sub (his mistake). So, when the pedicure units arrived on-site, the plumbing was not in place. Huge nightmare for the plumber—he had crews working nonstop over three days to run a new waste line with vent (code requires iron pipe in San Francisco) to the fourth floor! It occurred two weeks prior to the scheduled opening! $$$*

- *Because the location was in San Francisco, and on the fourth floor of a 1940s building, it was discovered that the concrete slab was not seismic built (with pre-stressed rebar). Had to redesign the casework and look at the total weight of all the equipment—and engineering was hired to work with retrofitting the space along with the equipment being modified. Huge cost and time. This occurred relatively early, but not for what needed to take place in order to make it happen! $$$$*

- *Lots of finger-pointing and lawsuits threatened (it is the American way, after all). Still, the place turned out stunning, industrial, and appropriate.*

- *A delay of four or five months beyond the initial targeted opening day and three $$$ big-buck cost overruns, equaling a final expenditure of $1.1 million. Place closed after one year. GAG!*

- *Same old adage: 'Plan for more time than initially told. Have more money than budgeted. Expect the unexpected.' I would add, focus on your project totally during its creation and stay as healthy as possible—the stress is immense!"*

CHAPTER 47

Good Reasons for Moving Your Salon

When you decide to do something as important as moving your business, there must always be a good enough reason for picking up stakes and planting new roots. For some, it may be a simple reason. For others, there are multiple factors. Listed below are the top reasons why businesses move. Where does your salon/spa fit in?

More Space

The most obvious example—the business has grown and is adding staff or additional services. The once-comfortable working space is no longer adequate for everyday business.

Another reason that crops up most often is the need to merge two businesses. The merge of the two businesses forces the owners to search for space to make conditions workable for clients and staff.

Owning Instead of Renting

In today's times, space is at an all-time high. For many business owners, the time comes when renting is no longer a viable financial option and buying becomes the only sensible thing to do. With rent on the upward trend, buying a place becomes more desirable. The potential threat of being squeezed out of your space or the constant rent increases will then be eliminated. Owning the building does bring on more responsibilities, such as: maintenance, finances, and ongoing upkeep. However, the most important benefit you have when you get ready to retire is that you can sell the business and property together or separately. It gives you a built-in RETIREMENT PLAN!

Changing Neighborhoods

As with most things, neighborhoods change and develop. Different circumstances may force you to relocate your salon.

The move may be the most important thing you do for your business. If the area is changing for the worse, your clients and staff will only welcome the move into a new environment. Be on the lookout for signs of neighborhood deterioration.

Relocating Near Home & School

Whether someone is from another state or even within the city, a move may be closer to home for convenience or necessity.

In some instances, moves made when parents find a school system that is more to their liking, moving to the suburbs, or finding solace in country locations. Business usually follows the same course within two years.

> **NOTE**
>
> Any move, no matter how well-planned, could result in the loss of clients and staff.

Business Divorce

For good or bad, richer or poorer, divorce or breaking up of a business/partnership is a predominant cause for a move.

When business partners split, the owners usually go their separate ways and find a new place to continue daily business. Keep in mind, even if the split is peaceful, clients and staff you thought were loyal may end up on the other side of the street.

Upgrading/Investment

As business prospers, many salon owners realize their need and desire to expand their location, or convert their salon to offer wellness or spa services. When searching for space, it pays to go a little bigger. If your growth has been on a continual climb, the new space will be inadequate within a short period. Moves are extremely costly. You do not want to do this every other year. When you plan new space, be certain to have some additional square footage for business growth over the short- and long-term.

Downgrading/Downsizing

Getting ready for retirement or being tired of managing a large staff may be reason enough to eliminate all those extra rooms and square footage. That is a common reason for businesses to move to a smaller space. It may also require eliminating other overhead expenses to finalize your plan and fit your revised budget.

Finally, even though you may believe you have adequate reasons to move, one would caution that this endeavor can be extremely complex and costly. The decision will require outside professionals to assist you with your ongoing relocation plans.

On the other hand, moving can be the most rewarding endeavor you accomplish in your business career. A well-planned move can benefit your business venture and revenues.

CHAPTER 48

Building Your Business to "Sell"

Y ou should always have a grasp on the value of your business. As business owners, there are many times when we have to face the perils of not knowing what's going to happen when Murphy's Law suddenly strikes. You may need to borrow money for the business quickly, transfer your company to a family member, sell a percentage to a deserving employee in your salon, or just sell your business outright. Many owners think the value is simply a multiple of earnings, but it's far from that.

Perhaps the best way to understand the value is to look at your business through the eyes of a potential buyer. It will enable you to see the key characteristics that influence the value of a business more clearly. Also, your accountant should give you a general idea of what your business is worth. Keep in mind, if you haven't been 100 percent honest with him, he will not be able to give you a true assessment. Here are a few things you should follow through the course of building your salon business.

Serve Niche Markets

Trying to be everything to everyone can blur a company's image and expose it to heavy competition. Instead, position the company as a market leader. Your salon should be known for its color or new, trendy, progressive styles. Focus on one or the other; it's hard to be good at both.

In a good market, you are often better off owning 60 percent of a niche then one percent of a broader market. Niche players have a sharp focus on a specific type of customer. They know their clientele down to the minute detail. Clients appreciated that because they know that they'll get exactly what they came in for—no surprises! You have superior service, expertise, and a product that fits their

NOTE

It's easier to sell a business with a niche than one that is a generalist.

needs, making your company more valuable. A prospective buyer looking to purchase your salon will understand this. They will realize there will be less chance for your clients to go to another salon if you should leave after the sale. They will be willing to pay extra for a salon business structure like this.

Sell Consumable Products

With consumable products, your first sale marks the beginning of a long relationship with your client and a steady stream of sales. Reorders are almost automatic and you shouldn't have high client turnover each year. Buyers and commercial banks look at retail as a steady stream of solid business income without the limitations of relying on the service side of the business. If you have a strong retail business, you automatically raise the bar on your selling price. To a bank or potential buyer, there is nothing stronger than a company with continual receivables.

> **NOTE**
> A strong retail base will get a higher price when selling the salon.

Build an Organization

A business that relies on only one or two people is worth far less to a bank or potential buyer than a company with a strong management team. Buyers don't like a one-man band. You may be the best owner/colorist in the business, but your business is only worth something if you continue as a worker after you sell. If the business relies on you to run it in order to bring in 75 percent of the sales, what is left if you leave the business?

Building a larger salon may mean you don't have as much control over every detail of the company. You must learn to relinquish some of the responsibilities to your staff. The growing process is very expensive and involves your time and dedication. Larger businesses are often more complex and harder to manage. The payoff, however, is not only better operating results, but a higher sale price for your company. In return, you'll have a trained and responsible management team that is stronger than other, smaller salons. They offer better market share, broader product lines, more assets, and greater capabilities.

Maintain Creditable Financial Statements

Financial statements provide a record of a company's operations and a statement of assets, liabilities, and more important, sales and profits. A true financial statement will give any would-be buyer or bank loan officer the confidence they need to purchase your salon business or to give your company a loan. The last thing a potential buyer or bank wants to hear is that you are keeping two sets of books or that you are not reporting everything your company earns. Foggy financials will cost you the sale or bank loan. A buyer loses faith in you and your company's credibility if he can't understand and have a high degree of confidence in its reports.

Remember, you may think you are a winner by not reporting all your income, but when the time comes to get a quick loan or sell your business, you will find it virtually impossible to do either.

Profits & Sales = Higher Price

Projecting results for a company with historical peaks and valleys in profits is very difficult. Potential buyers and banks will devalue a company with this type of performance. They may pass on buying or lending you money if this is the case. A salon with steady profits and sales will yield a much higher price than one that doesn't. It is important to keep your business numbers consistent.

Low Overhead & No Debt

Many salons are virtually impossible to sell for any net price, because the business debts exceed the gross value of the business. A seller may preach that his business makes a fortune, but the owner is consuming too much money, the business is consuming too much working capital, and a recent salon expansion or remodel that was undercapitalized has the company riddled with debt. If this is how your business is run, please be aware that you will not be able to sell or receive bank financing. Debt will scare away any potential buyer or loan officer.

If you are able to sell your business, the outstanding debt would be deducted from the gross purchase price. That may leave the seller with very little money at all. The key is to run a tight ship, keep overhead down, buy what you need, and don't over expand. A salon remodel is something that should be done every 5 years, but you should only remodel what is needed. Paint goes a long way. Save the money needed for the remodel before you even think about doing anything. The lack of business debt will make life easy for you and your salon and will be worth a lot more when you are thinking about selling.

Timeline

ONE YEAR (or more) BEFORE OPENING

- Look at the pros and cons of owning and operating your own salon
- Decide if you are ready
- Take the entrepreneurial self-test
- Will you buy an existing salon or start your own?
- Decide if you will rent booths

BUYING AN EXISTING SALON

- Analyze the operation
- Review financials
- Create a spreadsheet with projections and debt ratios
- Create a budget
- Make an offer to purchase
- Remodel the salon
- Hire an architect and contractor
- Determine your list priorities for coordination and timing
- Begin your transformation weekend

STARTING A NEW SALON

- Choose a business structure
- Name your salon
- Hire a lawyer

- Gather/apply for:
  EIN
  Articles of Incorporation
  Resolution
  Identification
- Pick a location for your new salon
- Complete the startup expense worksheet
- Work on your new business checklist: business plan and mission statement
- SECURE STARTUP FUNDS!!
- Negotiate your lease
- Find an equipment designer and architect
- Price your salon furniture
- Find your contractor
- Obtain licenses and permits:
  EIN (Employer Identification Number)
  Articles of Incorporation
  Resolution
  Identification
  Initial deposit
- Set up a business checking account
- Plan your signage
- Choose the colors of your salon
- Obtain business insurance for opening day of business
- Hire a bookkeeper and/or an accountant
- Design and develop web presence and determine social marketing strategy
- Decide on computers and software for your salon
- Choose a business phone system
- Write your employee manual
- Design and develop a salon menu
- Set up online promotions
- Choose which retail products to sell
- Begin to hire

WITHIN SIX MONTHS OF OPENING

- Plan salon promotions and loyalty programs
- Discreetly begin the hiring process

WITHIN THREE MONTHS OF OPENING

- Arrange for salon promotions and loyalty programs (negotiate with vendors, decide if you need loyalty cards, etc.)

WITHIN ONE MONTH OF OPENING

- Train staff on computer software and hardware

WITHIN TWO OR THREE WEEKS OF OPENING

- The controversial exit
- Preparing for the open house

AFTER OPENING

- Successful retail in year one
- Surviving the first year—what to expect and how to adjust
- Build your business to sell
- Moving your salon

Glossary

Build-out: estimate of the amount and location of potential development for an area.

Equity: the net value of assets minus liabilities.

Executive Summary: an overview of the main points of a business plan or proposal.

GM methodology: general merchandise methodology, or how you will purchase, display, and record your merchandise.

Lien: the legal claim of one person upon the property of another person to secure the payment of a debt or the satisfaction of an obligation.

Market-driven: determined by or responsive to market forces.

Noncompete Agreement: a contract that restricts participation in a certain market by a company or an individual under specific circumstances. Employers often require employees to sign a Noncompete Agreement to deter them from quitting and joining a competitor.

Point-of-Sale (POS): (also sometimes referred to as Point-of-Purchase [POP] or checkout) is the location where a transaction occurs. A "checkout" refers to a POS terminal, or more generally to the hardware and software used for checkouts, the equivalent of an electronic cash register.

Prorate: to make an arrangement on a basis of proportional distribution.

Reserve requirements or hold-backs: requirements regarding the amount of funds that banks must hold in reserve against deposits made by their customers. This money must be in the bank's vaults or at the closest Federal Reserve Bank.

Revenue stream: a form of revenue. Revenue streams refer specifically to the individual methods by which money comes into a company.

Search Engine Optimization (SEO): This is the process of improving the visibility of a website or Web pages in search engines via the "natural" or unpaid search results.

A **softphone** is a software program for making telephone calls over the Internet using a general purpose computer, rather than using dedicated hardware.

Twist-on wire connectors: used to fasten two or more electrical conductors together. They are a type of electrical connector.

Underwriter's Laboratory (UL): this company certifies electrical devices acceptable for use in the United States.

Index

Works Cited

"Cosmetologists of America for members of the beauty salon industry." *Cosmetologists of America.* Cosmetologists of America, n.d. Web. 25 Aug. 2011.

< http://www.cosmetologistsofamerica.com>.

"Facebook Statistics, Application Statistics, Page Statistics – Socialbakers." *Facebook Statistics, Application Statistics, Page Statistics – Socialbakers.* N.p., n.d. Web. 25 Aug. 2011.

<http://www.socialbakers.com/>.

"Inside Facebook – Tracking Facebook and the Facebook Platform for Developers and Marketers." *Inside Facebook – Tracking Facebook and the Facebook Platform for Developers and Marketers.* N.p., n.d. Web. 25 Aug. 2011.

<http://www.insidefacebook.com>.

"The U.S. Small Business Administration | SBA.gov." *The U.S. Small Business Administration | SBA.gov.* N.p., n.d. Web. 25 Aug. 2011.

<http://www.sba.gov >.

"U.S. Bureau of Labor Statistics." *U.S. Bureau of Labor Statistics.* N.p., n.d. Web. 25 Aug. 2011.

<http://www.bls.gov>.

Moran, Gwen. "Business & Small Business | News, Advice, Strategy | Entrepreneur.com." *Business & Small Business | News, Advice, Strategy | Entrepreneur.com.* N.p., n.d. Web. 11 Aug. 2011.

<http://www.entrepreneur.com>.

"Small Business Ideas and Resources for Entrepreneurs." *Small Business Ideas and Resources for Entrepreneurs.* N.p., n.d. Web. 19 Aug. 2011.

<**http://www.inc.com**>**.**

"The U.S. Small Business Administration | SBA.gov." *The U.S. Small Business Administration | SBA.gov.* N.p., n.d. Web. 15 Aug. 2011.

<**http://www.sba.gov**>**.**

"eHow | How to Videos, Articles & More - Discover the expert in you. | eHow.com." *eHow | How to Videos, Articles & More – Discover the expert in you. | eHow.com.* N.p., n.d. Web. 1 Aug. 2011.

<**http://www.ehow.com**>**.**

MLA formatting by BibMe.org.

Special Thanks

Jeff and Eric would like to especially thank and acknowledge
Patrick Parenty, L'Oreal, and their divisions for supporting Ready, Set, Go!
and helping to make this one-of-a-kind publication a reality!

Contributors & Resources

Jeff Grissler, Quest Resources, Salon Equipment Financing (jgrissler@questrs.com)

    questrs.com

John Harms, President/Founder Meevo (Millennium)

    meevo.com

Guy Wadas, National Sales Director, Integrity Payment Systems.

    integritypaymentsystems.com

Jill Krahn, Senior Vice President of Sales, The Salon Professional Academies Franchise Group

    thesalonprofessionalacademy.com

Kristi Valenzuela, Founder and Salon Success Coach, Crystal Focus Success Coaching.

    crystalfocus.com

Sales Professionals, Takara Belmont

    takarabelmont.com

Facebook Fans

Thank you for providing your stories and allowing us to share The Good, The Bad, &
The Ugly.*

*Quotes, provided via Facebook, were offered freely by salon owners and without obligation or compensation from Ready, Set, Go! Publishing, its authors, contributors, or endorsers. Quotes used in this book follow "fair use" practices with proper attribution given to those who submitted comments. When content is offered via a public domain, such as Facebook, it means that those posting or commenting are allowing their posts or comments to be shared, used, or accessed by people on and off of Facebook.

Follow Jeff Grissler & Eric David Ryant on Facebook

Image Sources

Takara Belmont

    takarabelmont.com

Peter Millard Designs

    millard-design.com

Rick Golden - Takara Belmont - Design Specialist

    rgolden@takarabelmont.com

Jeff Holmes - Takara Belmont - Regional Manager

    jholmes@takarabelmont.com

European Touch Pedicure Spas

    europeantouch.com

Blush Haus of Beaute

    blushhob.com

Minerva Beauty

    minervabeauty.com

Brian Donovan - etc. media

    etceteramedia.biz

Salon Centric Equipment Division

    saloncentric.com

Editors & Page Layout

Kelly Cobane Condron, Content Editing

Linda Demeshko, Copy Editing

Kim Campbell, Editor

Robin Krauss, Page Layout

MODERN
SALON

modernsalon.com

Receive the hottest and latest in beauty - live coverage, events, news, links to how-to education and photoshoots by connecting with us via our social media, e-Newsletters or magazines.

Connect with us ANYWHERE, ANYTIME

 facebook.com/ModernSalon

twitter.com/ModernSalon

pinterest.com/ModernSalon

Instagram.com/ModernSalon

For FREE trend updates, check the e-Newsletters you want to receive:
modernsalon.com/subscriben2014

If you do not have a print subscription yet, log on to:
modernsalon.com/subscribem2014

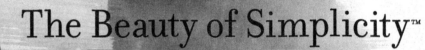

FIND YOUR STYLE TODAY | STYLING STATIONS | STYLING CHAIRS | SALON PACKAGES

CALL | EMAIL | CHAT

NORVELL®

THE INDUSTRY'S CHOICE
IN
PROFESSIONAL
SPRAY TANNING

     norvellsunless.com

LEGACY

*...more than just a chair...
...an experience.*

Turn heads with the clean lines and shiny chrome of a true classic — and look towards the future — with the Koken Legacy Chair by Takara Belmont. The masterfully crafted chair unites a traditional barbershop look-and-feel with the comforts of modern technology. Ergonomically engineered for barber and client alike, the Legacy features a variety of standard features and upgrades from backrest recline and synchronous footrest to towel hangers and a removable headrest.

Learn more: 1-800-526-3847
WWW.TAKARABELMONT.COM

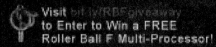

Visit bit.ly/RBFgiveaway
to Enter to Win a FREE
Roller Ball F Multi-Processor!

TAKARA BELMONT

TODAY. TOMORROW. ALWAYS.

DUET STYLING CHAIR

Pitch-ture Perfect.

The Duet Styling Chair by Takara Belmont makes a bold statement in chair design. With a pitch perfect harmony of durability, style and comfort, this little chair with a big voice offers a full cadence of notable features. The removable lumbar support cushion doubles as a booster seat to accommodate a family of clients and makes clean-up a breeze. Added steel reinforced back supports sets the stage for the Duet to complete an entire tour of services.

TODAY. TOMORROW. ALWAYS.

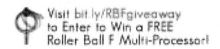

Visit bit.ly/RBFgiveaway
to Enter to Win a FREE
Roller Ball F Multi-Processor!

Learn more: 1-800-526-3847
WWW.TAKARABELMONT.COM

The *Future* is Now

ROLLER BALL *F*
Multi-Function Hair Processor

Visit http://bit.ly/RBFgiveaway
to Enter to Win a FREE
Roller Ball F Multi-Processor!

Advanced Technology

The original ROLLER BALL featured the
world's first infrared dome with a
rotating ring, offering an airiness and
smart processing style that you can't get
with hood-shaped hair processors.
We've now added more power and
style, creating a ROLLER BALL for a new
generation with an eye toward the
future—the ROLLER BALL F.

Think inside the bowl.

Black   Brown   White

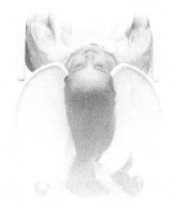

Offer your clientele more than just a standard service - provide them with a luxurious hair spa experience that will have them coming back for more.

Vibrant colors, lasting curls, and stronger wave length — the new Spa Mist II enhances salon treatments by generating a fine mist of microscopic water particles. It gently opens up the hair's cuticle layer for deep conditioning of the hair or scalp and allows for an added hand spa treatment. With a simple to use, light and portable design, the Spa Mist II from Takara Belmont delivers clients a truly relaxing facial for their hair.

Match a Spa Mist II with a shampoo unit from our new RSIII line for a deeply exhilarating spa shampoo service! Backwash shampoo units equipped with a deep bowl cut with the comfort of the stylist in mind, ultra-plush neck cushion, and ergonomically enhanced seating all add up to a uniquely relaxing shampoo experience – not just for the customer, but for the salon employees as well.

RS Elite   RS Prime   RS Luxis

Learn more: 1-800-526-3847
WWW.TAKARABELMONT.COM

Visit bit.ly/RBFgiveaway
to Enter to Win a FREE
Roller Ball F Multi-Processor!

TAKARA BELMONT

TODAY. TOMORROW. ALWAYS.

CPSIA information can be obtained at www.ICGtesting.com
Printed in the USA
BVOW07s1855040915

416507BV00009B/61/P